PRAISE FOR
inclusion UNCOMPLICATED

"Finally! A book about inclusion that everyone can understand and apply! Dr. White has written a brilliant, insightful, practical road map for creating an inclusive company. More importantly, she adds her unique insights and shares her practical experience working with her clients. This book is a must-read that combines common sense with Dr. White's firsthand personal experience, and it brings the reader back to the reality that transparent leadership and authentic people are the keys to inclusion. This is a must-read! If it comes to paying your mortgage or buying this book, let the bank wait!"

—DR. SHELTON J. GOODE
CEO, Icarus Consulting; Author, Beyond Inclusion: Reimagining the Future of Work, Workers, and the Workplace

"*Inclusion Uncomplicated* is an outstanding and trusted reference for anyone navigating the ever-changing world of diversity, equity, and inclusion. In this essential guide, Dr. Nika White brings a wealth of experience to explain these sometimes-complicated topics in an easy-to-understand way."

—AIKO BETHEA
Founder, RARE Coaching & Consulting

"When it comes to building a more inclusive workplace and world, the way forward can feel uncertain and overwhelmingly complex. Pulling on her over two decades in the DEI space, Nika has done a masterful job simplifying the key concepts we need to know and understand and laying out concrete actions each of us can take to make our contribution, regardless of our place in the change equation. This is a welcoming and nonjudgmental book that provides a ton of encouragement and support for all of us on our journeys!"

—JENNIFER BROWN

Founder and CEO, Jennifer Brown Consulting; Best-Selling Author,
Inclusion, How to be an Inclusive Leader, *and* Beyond Diversity
(with Rohit Bhargava)

"Being inclusive should not be another item on the to-do list. To be inclusive is to be human. Dr. White's work helps us all understand our collective role in creating positive change."

—JULIE KRATZ

Chief Engagement Officer, Next Pivot Point

"At this point in our collective history, we must move beyond conversations on diversity, equity, and inclusion into sustainable actions and meaningful transformation. There must be a clear path through the maze of new terminologies, acronyms, and trainings thrown at us daily. Dr. Nika's book provides a simplified approach to creating inclusive environments where everyone has a role to play and the opportunity to thrive."

—SACHA THOMPSON

Founder and Chief Inclusive Culture Curator, The Equity Equation

"*Inclusion Uncomplicated* is an honest and informative approach to the realm of diversity, equity, and inclusion. The lessons within will not only guide you in your work but also in everyday life."

—JARED KAROL

Author, A White Guy Confronting Racism: An Invitation to Reflect and Act

"The phenomenal and values-driven Dr. Nika White again illustrates the power of her trademark intentional inclusionist philosophy. As we are all keepers of the culture, we all have a responsibility and crucial role to play in realizing greater levels of inclusion, equity, and belonging. Dr. Nika White has dedicated herself to uplifting and protecting others, with a particular focus on the Black community, which she herself is part of. Through this book and all the work she does, she inspires many and significantly contributes to the transformative change that will make the world a more inclusive and equitable place to live in. Faith, Hope, and Love in Action!"

—MAIKEL GROENEWOUD

Manager Data Science & AI and Technology & Ethics, EY

"With *Inclusion Uncomplicated*, Dr. Nika White offers readers an essential guide to understanding the world around us and the people we interact with. In our increasingly global world, DEI is more important than ever."

—JIL LITTLEJOHN BOSTICK

Head of DEI, Winnebago Industries

"Dr. Nika White does an amazing job of untangling the often-complex nature of DEI to identify the common threads that hinder individuals and organizations from achieving their goals. She doesn't stop there. She artfully identifies the threads that enable us to feel a sense of belonging in both our personal and professional lives. As you read the examples she provides and engage with the critical reflection tools, this book will move you forward on your journey toward simplifying DEI."

—DR. PASCAL LOSAMBE

Cofounder and Chief Content Officer, Synergy Consulting Company

"Dr. Nika White is a genuine thought leader in diversity, equity, and inclusion, and with this book, she unravels the complex topic with care, intention, and determination. Read *Inclusion Uncomplicated*, and discover how you can play a role in this important progress."

—JENN TARDY

Founder and CEO, Jennifer Tardy Consulting

"Those familiar with Dr. Nika White's work know she consistently offers thoughtful and pragmatic advice. *Inclusion Uncomplicated* is an outstanding and trusted reference for anyone navigating the ever-changing world of diversity, equity, and inclusion. With her wealth of experience, Dr. White explains sometimes-complicated topics in an easy-to-understand way."

—WADE A. HINTON, ESQ.

CEO and Founder, Hinton & Company

"Dr. Nika White's *Inclusion Uncomplicated* is a powerful invitation to reflect more deeply on the role you are playing in creating a more inclusive and equitable world and how to increase your impact. She walks alongside you, creating pathways and expanding perspectives to help you move from the sidelines to the front line. *Inclusion Uncomplicated* is a road map to move from caution and comfort to curiosity and courage."

—SARAH NOLL WILSON

Author, Don't Feed the Elephants; *CEO, Sarah Noll Wilson, Inc.*

"Dr. Nika White holds nothing back in her goal of simplifying DEI. *Inclusion Uncomplicated* will challenge you to reflect on your own actions and the impact we have on others in our efforts to be more inclusive leaders. You may face an uncomfortable reality within, but these difficult topics must be discussed in the pursuit of progress. A must-read!"

—RAVEN SOLOMON

DEI Speaker, Author, and Strategist, Raven Solomon Enterprises

"*Inclusion Uncomplicated* is a welcome addition to my DEI bookshelf. Dr. White transforms the otherwise somewhat complex topic of inclusion into meaningful, straightforward steps. It's a journey you'll want to take."

—KAREN CATLIN

Author, Better Allies

"Dr. Nika White is one of the most compassionate, emotionally intelligent, capable, and insightful DEI practitioners I've had the privilege of partnering with and getting to know as a mentor and peer. She's got a knack for breaking down even the most complicated DEI concepts into tangible action steps in a way that makes you feel fired up and ready to go. With the DEI industry growing in scope and complexity, *Inclusion Uncomplicated* takes the best of Nika's hard-won wisdom across industries and organizations to empower equity-minded leaders to keep leading the charge while highlighting the need for all of us to play a role in creating more equitable organizations."

—KAY FABELLA

Cross-Cultural DEI Consultant and CEO, Inclusion in Progress, LLC

"Nika White is a thought leader in the diversity, equity, and inclusion (DEI) space. In this latest book, she demystifies DEI concepts so that leaders, champions, changemakers, and allies can leverage practical, actionable tools to create the biggest impact within their sphere of influence. If you're looking to increase your understanding and become more intentional about amplifying your impact as an inclusive, equitable leader in your community, team, and/or organization, I highly recommend *Inclusion Uncomplicated.*"

—ANU MANDAPATI

Global Diversity, Equity, and Inclusion Executive, IMPACT Leadership Partners

inclusion
UNCOMPLICATED

DR. NIKA WHITE

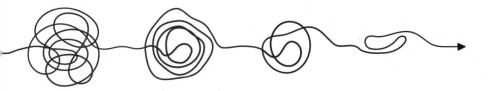

inclusion
UNCOMPLICATED

A TRANSFORMATIVE GUIDE TO SIMPLIFY DEI

Forbes | Books

Published by Forbes Books, Charleston, South Carolina.
Member of Advantage Media.

Forbes Books is a registered trademark, and the Forbes Books colophon is a trademark of Forbes Media, LLC.

Printed in the United States of America.

10 9 8 7 6 5 4 3 2 1

ISBN: 978-1-955884-15-0 (Hardcover)
ISBN: 978-1-955884-82-2 (eBook)
LCCN: 2022913676

Book design by Analisa Smith.
Creative direction by Peculiar LLC.
Photography by Stacey Gardin, Stacey Gardin Portraits.

This custom publication is intended to provide accurate information and the opinions of the author in regard to the subject matter covered. It is sold with the understanding that the publisher, Forbes Books, is not engaged in rendering legal, financial, or professional services of any kind. If legal advice or other expert assistance is required, the reader is advised to seek the services of a competent professional.

Since 1917, Forbes has remained steadfast in its mission to serve as the defining voice of entrepreneurial capitalism. Forbes Books, launched in 2016 through a partnership with Advantage Media, furthers that aim by helping business and thought leaders bring their stories, passion, and knowledge to the forefront in custom books. Opinions expressed by Forbes Books authors are their own. To be considered for publication, please visit **books.Forbes.com**.

To my husband, Carlo, for his relentless support and belief in my abilities to engage deeply in purpose-filled work of centering humanity and inclusion. To my beloved daughter, Hannah, and son, CJ, who inspire me daily to make this world a more inclusive place so they can always feel seen and valued and experience full opportunity.

Contents

Introduction

Leave no one behind is more than just a phrase or affirmation to reflect upon. This organizing principle drives every aspect of my leadership in the diversity, equity, and inclusion (DEI) field and is embedded in the ways I show up personally and professionally to do this critical work.

As an award-winning leadership consultant, entrepreneur, Black woman, and devoted mother of a neurodivergent son and a strong activist daughter, I consider DEI to be much more than a career choice. On one hand, it is my lived experience as a multigenerational minority within a dominant culture that systematically disadvantages people like me. On the other, it is within that same dominant system that I became an educated global expert because of college-focused parents and a commitment to generational wealth.

This unique perspective enables me to understand conditions within both dominant and nondominant cultures. I've inhabited both all my life and can now tease out parts of the systems and entrenched beliefs that get us all knotted up, frayed, and disoriented inside and out. It is in the act of fully unraveling the yarn—straightening and pulling taut the raw fibers that bind humanity in belongingness—that we remember we are intertwined. Interdependent.

Consider this: If you pull the working yarn from the center of the skein instead of from the outside, the ball of yarn will stay put. No matter how much you unwind it, it won't roll around. You can unravel the yarn at your own pace and prevent a tangled mess. That is what this book aims to do—to unravel DEI slowly and carefully, smoothing out confusion and simplifying the process.

I have deep convictions about the work of DEI. It is a calling, a ministry, as well as my career. I believe that DEI is not just a check mark for good business. It's a way to transform the world.

I am not into shame/blame/judgment; rather, I am into building bridges of understanding.

Amid all the noise and anger and finger pointing, I bring a perspective of trying to bridge the knowledge gap. Not to alienate people but to help them and compel them to join the DEI journey, the journey toward a more transformational humanity. In essence, I am inviting people to tap into their greatest selves.

I shared the yarn tip because when I think of the challenges surrounding DEI, I want people to unravel the big ball of yarn of complexity that binds us together. This creates space for us to begin the true work of weaving a more inclusive and equitable future.

The themes we will explore in this book mirror the greater "undoing" already set in motion since 2020–2021 after the murder of George Floyd by a Minneapolis police officer and the blatant racial disparities that surfaced during the COVID-19 pandemic.

Public outcry sounded the alarm—enough was enough—fueling mass awareness and social media movements that demanded corporations and society at large to proactively address systemic racism. Compliance-oriented diversity training has existed within large corporations since the 1980s, but DEI has now become a mainstream buzzword and an $8 billion industry.[1]

While these highly publicized events heightened awareness and inspired momentum, they also created a surge of self-ascribed DEI experts with little or no experience. You can feel confident that the wisdom contained in this book has been decades in the making. Each of the lessons, learnings, and helpful techniques comes from my more than twenty years of experience as an antiracism leader, an advocate, and a weaver of systems to promote equity for all.

DEI is seen as the most viable solution to educate white corporate culture and to actively address, measure, and make amends for inequities built into the historical mistreatment of diverse minority populations. Yet, despite corporate America's $50 billion promise in racial justice pledges in 2021 (which included new hiring policies and practices, DEI officers, and implicit bias trainings), the equity dial has barely moved.[2]

The reasons for this are complicated and varied. Sometimes it's because the manager in charge, despite best intentions, cannot see beyond a limited perspective. Sometimes companies get derailed in semantics and classifications instead of real-world human outcomes. Other times it's performative: a company checks a box while checking out on employees' needs to feel safe or to receive equal pay. Many corporations have learned the hard way that forcing obligatory training onto employees who don't want it in the first place ends up reinforcing negative biases and harms the populations it aims to protect.[3]

By far, however, resistance and lack of progress can be traced to one thing: DEI is viewed as overwhelming and downright confusing. There are myriad ways to describe, to deliver, and to measure this important work. And there are many paths to get there, with varying degrees of success. Whether you are a newcomer or have been immersed in DEI for a while, unraveling each dimension of this work requires a trusted guide to knead the knots and loosen the tangles that seem impossible to get through.

DEI is complicated, but it doesn't have to feel that way. My primary reason for writing this book, *Inclusion Uncomplicated,* is to demystify DEI concepts so that leaders, champions, and changemakers like you can own practical, actionable tools to make a real difference, right now.

The heart of my work is to help create transformative environments with intentionality around inclusion. This book will teach you how to do that, personally and professionally. I have worked with more than two hundred corporate, educational, government, and nonprofit brands and managed over $200 million in business assets. I am also a sought-after keynote speaker on team engagement, organizational leadership, strategic diversity, race equity, and intentional inclusion.

In the chapters ahead, you will find concrete advice and easy-to-follow steps that I've developed from more than twenty years in DEI leadership. *I've defined the number one barrier to DEI success, detailed steps that guarantee inclusion, shared common organizational mistakes, and revealed unexpected opportunities.* You will learn from real-life

---

3   Tiffany Green and Nao Hagiwara, "The Problem with Implicit Bias Training," *Scientific American*, August 28, 2020, accessed June 4, 2022, https://www.scientificamerican.com/article/the-problem-with-implicit-bias-training/.

workplace mistakes and successes, hear revealing stories from diverse voices, and upgrade your skill set to contribute to systems change.

Think of this as a trusted guide you can return to at any time to avoid common pitfalls, to navigate through tricky situations, and to show up intentionally so action equals impact. As you needle through each page, you'll undo learned behaviors that entangle us in webs of racism, discrimination, and confusion.

What Is **DEI**?

Before we dive in, it's important to level set some basic terms and expectations.

When we talk about the work of DEI, we mean people at the table who have the wherewithal, the influence, and the power to be able to create opportunities of equity for those who are historically marginalized and disenfranchised. This includes women, minorities, people of color, LGBTQ+, the neurodivergent, and individuals with varying physical abilities.

Diversity is often misunderstood. The term simply describes a point of respect in which things differ. Historically, this was all about tolerance for people who are different from us. Yet people don't want to be just tolerated. They want to be valued, celebrated, and seen as key contributors and to have full opportunity for success. Diversity doesn't need us to do anything for it to exist. It's already here and happening.

> **We can't be passive about the work of inclusion. We must be intentional.**

Inclusion is all about action. This means we are being strategic, action oriented, and calculated in trying to help create belonging. And we can't be passive about the work of inclusion. We must be intentional. We will speak a lot about intention and its role in inclusion throughout our journey.

Equity gets us to our destination. If equality for all people is still the hoped-for end—which it is—then equity is how we're going to get there. We have to level the playing field. However, equity is often associated with affirmative action, and people assume if they lean into the idea of opportunities for all, they must lose something in the process. In the words of attorney and civil rights advocate Angela Glover, "Equity is not a zero-sum game."[4] We all benefit from equity. To center equity is to center justice.

It Starts with You

Inclusion Uncomplicated is destined to become a transformational journey because it inspires change from the inside out, beginning with the individual. There are countless books available to address organizational structure, company practices, and metrics. I will include practical tips where applicable, but the purpose of *Inclusion Uncomplicated* is not more mechanics.

The goal is behavioral change.

When I say *behavioral change*, it could be you're already doing this work and want to take it to the next level. Or it could be that your behavior is now operating against the work of inclusivity, belonging, and equity, so you have a whole runway of opportunity to improve. This book will better equip you for what's ahead no matter your starting point.

Change occurs on an individual level, or it doesn't occur at all. Companies are made up of individuals. Individuals model inclusive

---

4   Angela Glover Blackwell, "The Curb-Cut Effect," *Stanford Social Innovation Review*, Winter 2017, accessed June 4, 2022, https://www.policylink.org/aboutUs/staff/angela-glover-blackwell.

behaviors and open doors of opportunity for others. If we cannot integrate this mindset on a personal level, then organizations—and ultimately society—will lack scaffolding to build sustainable structures.

Inclusive environments begin with each of us showing up and doing our part. People who carry the title of chief diversity officer, or manager, or director, or even human resources professional should not be expected to carry the burden alone. This is something for all of us to carry.

Every one of us has a sphere of influence. It could be within our family, within our workplace, within our teams, within our community, within our church. No matter your role or title—you are a leader by influence. To substantiate this claim, Yale researchers concluded that our behaviors directly influence up to three degrees of friendship.[5] That means the friend of your friend's friend is influenced by what you do and say, even if you've never met! Your level of responsibility and commitment as an ally will have a ripple effect and inspire others along the way.

Without a collective shift in the way we relate to one another as humans, without willingness to recognize our personal biases or to withhold assumptions and sit with the discomfort, systems of oppression will remain locked in place. This book helps us all get there together—from personal transformation to organizational change and societal impact.

As you dog-ear these pages in the coming days, you will discover I do not believe in shame, blame, or guilt. I do believe in education and accountability in illuminating the path and saying what is true. It takes courage. It takes tools. It takes patience, practice, and persever-

---

5 James H. Fowler and Nicholas A. Christakis, "Dynamic spread of happiness in a large social network: longitudinal analysis over 20 years in the Framingham Heart Study," BMJ, December 5, 2008, https://doi.org/10.1136/bmj.a2338.

ance. It's my hope this book will be a worthy companion and a trusted guide on your DEI journey.

How to Use This Book

Because I have made no assumptions about where readers are on the DEI path, this book is organized in the simplest, most accessible way. Each chapter introduces certain key concepts, provides definitions and real-life scenarios, and ends with a set of prompts called "Critical Reflection."

Critical reflection is a "meaning-making process" that helps us set goals, use what we've learned in the past to inform future action, and consider the real-life implications of our thinking. It is the link between thinking and doing, and at its best, it can be transformative.

I encourage you to take notes and, most especially, to take time to pause for introspection and honest reflection. Respond to each prompt no matter what it brings up for you.

This is a big part of my philosophy and how I show up to this space. I never facilitate sessions where some intentional time for people to reflect and to process together has not been built in. *What did I hear? How do I feel about what I heard? What do I plan to do with it? What curiosities are still coming up?* That's part of how we show up to this work.

It will also help to digest new perspectives, to consider real-life implications, and to set actionable goals in the near-term and long-term future.

Transformative learning involves transformation in three dimensions: psychological changes in the understanding of the self, convictional revision of belief systems, and behavioral changes in lifestyle/actions. As you go along, please consider the following dimensions:

- ⚈ **PSYCHOLOGICAL:** How have the contents of each chapter helped you to understand yourself?

- ⚈ **CONVICTIONAL:** How has the material you learned changed your belief systems?

- ⚈ **BEHAVIORAL:** How has this new information changed your lifestyle/actions?

A truly transformational journey requires making a link between thinking and doing. This book offers you all the structure, education, and practical tools you'll need—but only you can bring the willingness, the commitment, and the action to make this a life-changing endeavor.

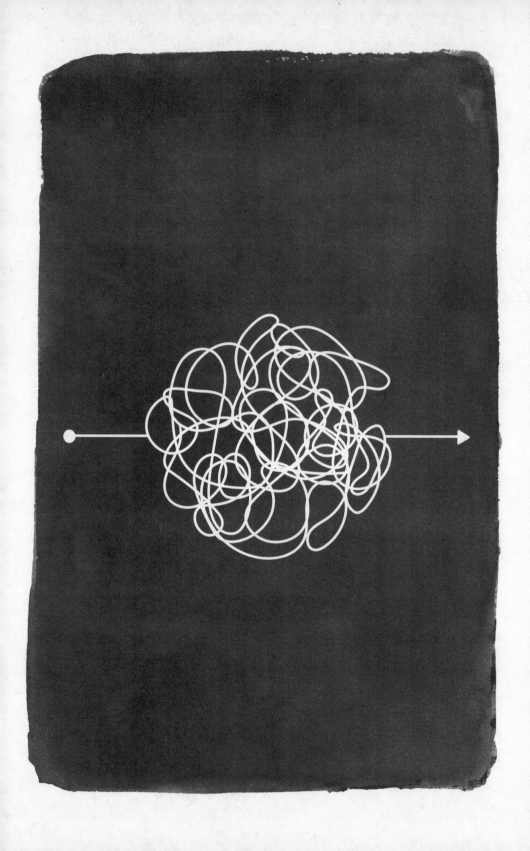

CHAPTER 1:

Inclusion Is a Mindset

The most common way people give up their
power is by thinking they don't have any.

—ALICE WALKER

My background is in marketing communications, and I was working for an advertising agency years ago. I really thought that I was going to be in that space for the long haul. I enjoyed everything about it. The agency environment is fast paced, dynamic, and I remember sitting in my office one day thinking about how much I love this culture and this environment. Always on time, on budget, on strategy.

The agency that I worked for happened to have been head-quartered in Greenville, South Carolina, but it also had an office in New York. I had the good fortune of being able to go back and forth between offices. I was always so envious of the New York office because, relative to South Carolina, it was a much more diverse workforce.

I began to think about the work of marketing communications professionals, advertising agency professionals, and the fact that our job is to be smart partners to our clients and to help reach a diverse America with their messages. I just wondered that if I loved this career so much, why weren't there others that looked like me taking advantage of this career path? I couldn't let that go.

I remember going to the president/CEO of the agency, whom I had a really good rapport with at the time. The agency employed about four hundred or more people, but he was very accessible. I talked to him about my affinity for the agency and for the work. I shared that I knew that at the time, our BHAG (the Big, Hairy, Audacious Goal) was to be the most admired agency.

What I also knew is that agencies in New York, because New York is the advertising capital of the world, had the attorney general contacting their offices and other key leaders saying, "We have to diversify. This is not a suggestion. It's a mandate, because our industry depends upon it." But no one was thinking about the agencies and other markets outside Greenville or outside New York because those other markets weren't known for that type of industry.

I said, "If we want to be the most admired agency, why are we waiting for someone to knock on our door and tell us what we need to do that's going to help us be a much smarter partner to our clients? We need to be much more intentional in how we are diversifying our workforce. The business depends upon it. Our clients rely on it, and I just wanted to share these thoughts."

He listened very intently, asked some very thought-provoking questions. I was prepared for all of them except the last one, which was, "Nika, I agree. We're going to do it. You're going to lead it. Now tell me—how?"

It was just one person seeing an opportunity for inclusion where there was a gap. I knew it would be instrumental and that leaning into it would catapult us into becoming a strong and healthy organization.

That was years ago, and I did not know that was going to be the start of my true trajectory: working full time in the DEI space, which has led to so many other opportunities. You do not have to wait for someone in a leadership role to say we're going to do this. If you see something, say something.

DEI has become an overused acronym that organizations employ to untangle the knots: knots created by complex cultural classifications, knots of historical injustice, and knots of social reckoning that must be realized so we can rebuild society, intentionally and inclusively.

DEI has also become shorthand for a process that can feel mystical or unattainable. Many people stay on the sidelines and become passive—not because they don't care but because they don't understand the value or they don't know what to do. We might assume they are against DEI and belonging because we sense resistance, so we try to cancel, shame, guilt, or blame them. But that's not getting us to where we want to go.

You do not have to wait for someone in a leadership role to say we're going to do this. If you see something, say something.

What will? *Recognizing that resistance is often just a lack of clarity.* Lack of clarity is not right, wrong, good, bad—it just is. It's also easily fixable. The best way to address that resistance and bring people onboard, however, is a topic of big discussion within the DEI space.

Practitioners are questioning, "When is it time to stop meeting people where they are and to more assertively pull them along?" The criticism is that meeting people where they are centers whiteness/ dominant culture and works to make white people comfortable at the expense of marginalized groups. So, the question becomes: "How do we educate in the most effective way? How do we build rapport, tell stories, and model inclusive behavior?"

While there are no singular answers to these questions—DEI is a journey, after all—by picking up this book, you're already on your way to becoming more intentional, courageous, and committed.

I often hear newcomers on the journey say, "What if I don't do it right?" or "What if I get called out?" instead of thinking about it as getting *called in*, which is a growth opportunity. That's the difference. True inclusion requires us to change our mindset.

The word *mindset* refers to an established set of attitudes held by a person, and we form those attitudes through a complex blend of family and peer influences, life experiences, genetics, economics, education, personality, and more. Thanks to evolutionary processes, our brains automatically prefer people who look, think, and act like we do (known as in-group preference or implicit bias). So, to step fully into inclusion, we must be prepared to shift those instinctual impulses that keep us trapped in what is exclusive and familiar. We literally must retrain our brains to move beyond our natural limited thinking.

How do we arrive at an inclusion mindset? We begin by knitting together a new fabric of understanding of who we are together, as humanity:

- **We are more similar than not.** Humans are 99.9 percent genetically identical.[6] Despite this scientific fact, within societies across the globe, in our offices, in our communities,

---

6   National Human Genome Research Institute (NHGRI), "Whole Genome Associa-
     tion Studies," NHGRI, July 15, 2011, accessed June 4, 2022, https://www.genome.
     gov/17516714/2006-release-about-whole-genome-association-studies.

and even within our own families, our differences receive the most attention. We are made of the same yarn—DNA—but we have different colors, textures, and expressions.

● **Inclusion recognizes that all people are entitled to humanity and to dignity. Every voice matters. Every person contributes value.** At one time or another, each of us has felt rejected, exploited, or completely invisible. For certain populations, however, these are not isolated occurrences—they are everyday, common experiences due to historic systems of oppression within employment, healthcare, and social structures. Some strands of culture have been much more frayed, separated, and diminished than others.

● **DEI is everyone's responsibility.** DEI belongs to all of us and is something we should all care about. It is not just the job of leaders, managers, or activists on the front lines to create systemic change. Our outcomes and collective futures are forever intertwined.

● **Race and gender are cultural concepts, not biological facts.** Society created classifications for purposes of capitalism and census. We all wear identity labels according to our placement within or outside dominant culture; some identities are self-ascribed (placed on us by society, which we may or may not accept), and others are self-avowed (owned by our choosing). Some threads feel authentic while others feel synthetic.

● **DEI is a lot more than race and gender.** It includes people with varying degrees of physical ability, neurodivergence, illness, sexual preference, economics, trauma, and more. While we do have to attack the optics of race and gender—because they are the most obvious to address in any organization—we remain inclusive of all who diverge from the dominant cultural norm. Every thread fortifies the whole.

- **Diversity is necessary for survival.** This is true in all aspects of the natural world and in the human family. Making the mindset leap from considering DEI an obligation to seeing it as a great opportunity is part of the necessary paradigm shift. Diversity creates strength, beauty, and resilience.

- **DEI work doesn't imply that white people have not had any burdens or hardships.**[7] It just means that the color of their skin is not the reason for those burdens or hardships. We must acknowledge this fact along with racial equity and help people to unpack and understand the historical context of race.

- **There's no one way to get there**. People receive and learn in different ways. There is no singular modality to bring every person into the DEI camp. We all respond to different patterns.

- **There is no finish line: DEI is a dynamic, transformational journey.** We are all going to make mistakes, but we're still going to show up prepared and take opportunities to keep doing better. Those of us who are champions know our work is not necessarily to get people to the finish line, whatever that looks like, because there is no finish line. Perhaps we only plant the seed, and then someone else comes

---

7   The capitalization of *Black*, especially in the context of this DEI book, is to help center the fact that Black people have been marginalized. The capitalization, to me, helps to further the point of changing that narrative. White people, as the dominant culture, haven't been subjected to systems of oppression due to race.

behind and nurtures that seed. Then something else they're exposed to, whether it's a film or a book or a meme or a talk, further nurtures the seed, and it starts to grow. No matter how we further the work, it helps people expand and creates positive change. No effort is ever wasted. Every little action makes a difference. Weaving transformation is the epic work of our lifetimes.

DEI *Gets Personal*

Adopting the inclusion mindset is a practical shift that is going to enrich, empower, and ultimately transform every person in your organization—beginning with you. Like any meaningful journey, the path to inclusion begins with figuring out your starting point, your location in the DEI landscape.

AWARENESS AND REFLECTION

We are so set on making definitive statements that we don't spend enough time on asking thoughtful questions first. That's part of simplifying DEI. We don't know what we don't know. Your starting location—the ideas, beliefs, assumptions, and behaviors you hold around DEI and about others who look, think, and act differently than you do—is ground zero. We cannot show up fully to this work and understand others if we have no clue about ourselves.

Let this first step be a curious one! As you explore the following concepts, pause with each new idea, and check in with yourself. What is your immediate reaction? Do you find yourself drawn to certain ideas while rejecting others? Are your thoughts becoming defensive, excited, discounting, shaming? Do you think that what you're reading doesn't apply to you or that you're the only one who keeps getting it wrong?

Notice when you feel conflict, sadness, confusion, anger, joy, overwhelm, relief, whatever. Then stop. Ask yourself questions such as the following: "Where is this coming from? Does this remind me of something from my past? What emotion am I feeling? Where is the emotion stuck in my body? What do I need to do, say, or let go of? Is there someone I need to make amends with? What needs to change, right here, right now? What unknowns or curiosities am I holding that I need to investigate?"

These are all examples of self-awareness and self-reflection—the foundational tools that build inclusion from the inside out. True inclusion cannot happen with others unless we begin with ourselves.

BE INTENTIONAL

Intentionality is the separator from those who are just going through the DEI motions versus those who are getting results and having an impact. Inclusion is all about action—being strategic and calculated and helping to create inclusive outcomes. You can't be passive about the work of inclusion. You must be intentional.

RECOGNIZE THAT PASSIVITY IS A BARRIER TO CHANGE

Understand that your passivity is perpetuating the problem. Passivity keeps our society from being able to fully optimize belonging—where no one is left behind, and we all benefit as a result.

Perhaps you are coming from a place of not having lived experiences and have chosen to remain neutral—not because you don't believe the work is valuable but because it just hasn't impacted you.

The moment you realize that you have been passive, you create an opportunity to shift that behavior.

As I've mentioned, people choose to be passive for different reasons, and it's often just a lack of clarity. Get clear on why you want to show up to this work. Explore ways to contribute, and define what actions you plan to take. I'll help you actualize those steps in upcoming chapters on storytelling, bias, and allyship.

BE OPEN

Be open to what you don't see and to what's not naturally coming up for you. Stay willing to learn from circumstances, ways of thinking, and lived experiences that are unfamiliar. When you are exposed to different thoughts, really let them permeate in a way that causes you to feel a call to action in some capacity.

FOLLOW THE CALL TO ACTION

Perhaps you're here because you want to dig deeper or go further. Maybe you want to be on a personal learning journey where you unravel some pesky knots of your own and gain more perspective before taking a strong stance in one area. Follow that inclination. Embrace and appreciate the incremental steps, and trust the unfolding journey.

UNDERSTAND THAT EVERYONE HAS BIAS

Regardless of who we are, what demographic we belong to, or what our upbringing has been, we have bias. It's human, but it's no excuse for prejudice, discrimination, or racism. We each have a record inside us since birth, and everything that we've been exposed to is stored on that record. It doesn't keep track of right, wrong, good, or bad. It's just a record. We have been influenced by everything that has surrounded us—our families, relationships, media, and organizations and institutions we've been a part of.

Self-awareness and self-reflection (once again) will be your best tools in figuring out how to mitigate that bias from creating harm to others. For example, ask yourself the following: "What are my personal prejudices or the personal stereotypes I gravitate toward?" Interrogate those thoughts. Why do they exist? Where are they coming from?

When people pause to trace back in time, they often realize they're projecting some past isolated incident onto the present moment. A commitment to inclusion means intentionally slowing down and staying aware when our behaviors don't match the situation. When those thoughts arise, it's about being mindful enough to pause and literally say, "Wait a minute. Let me self-reflect." That gives you space and time to interpret what is really happening. Is it valid? Is it coming from a place of bias?

We cannot allow past experiences to impact decision-making about the present-moment people and situations we encounter. It's unwarranted, and it causes damage. Bias makes us human, but it does not exonerate us from our actions. Knowing our biases ahead of time allows us to be aware of go-tos, triggers, and inaccurate assumptions and to consciously course correct.

CHOOSE COURAGE OVER COMFORT

Be willing to be uncomfortable. Acknowledge the discomfort that comes for someone who's on this journey, and know it will get hard at times if you're truly committed to systems change. Understand that we are all going to make mistakes and will continue to learn with each new encounter. That's what being an ally and a changemaker is about.

ACTIVELY SEEK MORE INFORMATION

We often expect information to come to us organically, or we may rely on our professional circles or place of employment to help educate us on these topics. Sometimes we don't take enough time to own our personal learning journey. What else are you doing to supplement that learning?

LOOK FOR THE EVIDENCE

A lot of people say they care about DEI, but they see it as someone else's responsibility. They may remark on how proud they are to be part of an organization that values inclusion. My question is this: What do you do? What do you do to help foster the culture they're trying to build? How do you show up with inclusive behaviors? How do you help elevate the level of thinking and behaviors within the organization to lean more into this whole lens of inclusiveness?

Remember, people are the ones who are running the organizations, who are running society, who are managing their families and building relationships. That can't be missed. Sometimes people do see the broad work of DEI as something specific to an organizational structure and that it has a strong place there, but how does that get infiltrated? Through the people.

If an individual or organization is touting leadership and commitment and valuing diversity, equity, inclusion, and belonging, where's the evidence behind that? Evidence is tied to the optics. Right, wrong, or indifferent, have impact by being seen as someone who is credible. Be that person who is exercising rigor to ensure they are—and others are—delivering upon that message.

Identifying the Mental Models of **DEI**

As individuals, we each have our own reasons behind how or why we engage in the work of diversity, equity, and inclusion. While some of us may be far along in our DEI journey, others are just now joining the conversation. To better understand someone's lens and perspectives concerning DEI, it benefits us to know an individual's mental model. Understanding mental models prepares DEI champions and allies to increase the likelihood of others engaging in inclusive leadership practices. Because mental models can vary, here is a breakdown of a few examples and signs to help identify them.

PERSONAS

Active Opposition

Active opposers are typically deeply rooted in their choice to be a strong opponent of DEI. These are the people whose minds cannot be changed and who are committed to disrupting the work of DEI. The potential for engagement is slim and often leads to the determination that the energy of trying is in vain. My advice is to let them be—there are far too many other people who can be persuaded. Putting our energy into changing the minds of active opposers can cause burnout. The best way to interact with these individuals is to not engage in heated conversation and to show them love in the best way you can, not hate. In the wise words of Dr. Martin Luther King Jr., "I have decided to stick with love. Hate is too great a burden to bear." Light drives out darkness.

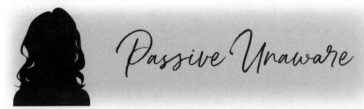

Passive Unaware

These are the people who are unaware and cannot engage in the work of DEI, simply because they are uninformed. Passively unaware individuals can be identified by their lack of engagement in the conversation and their inability to recognize the severity of the problems that loom of equity and equality.

If you notice a group discussing the lack of Brown and Black people on a panel, and this person doesn't engage, bring them into the conversation. After getting them to the discussion, if they share, they don't have much to add to the subject or don't have the point of view to weigh in; we can infer that they are passively unaware. This is an opportunity to connect and expose the individual to broader perspective. Reach out to have a one-on-one conversation. Ask questions, share your personal investment in DEI, and listen. Make sure to listen to learn.

Passively aware individuals are the ones who can appreciate that attention is being given to the work of DEI but see it as someone else's responsibility—the bystander effect. To illustrate passive awareness, we can use the same situation from passive unawareness.

If you notice a group discussing the lack of Brown and Black people on a panel and this person doesn't engage, bring them into the conversation. After getting them to the discussion, if they express that they realize DEI is essential but trust other people to get the job done, you can recognize passive awareness.

They see this as the work of someone else instead of taking ownership to help solve inequity. Often this disengagement comes from feeling that DEI is about marginalized communities. If someone doesn't identify with a marginalized community, they may be dismissive about their personal accountability.

Because this person is aware of the need to value DEI, they can be persuaded to deepen their engagement and begin to see themselves as part of the solution. Meet them where they are. Invite them for coffee or tea, and have a chat. Ask them questions to suggest entry points of engagement in DEI that feel comfortable to them as they start an intentional journey of modeling inclusive leadership. This is an opportunity to show them their voice matters. They can serve as an ally and be an advocate for change for those in their circle of influence.

Our actively aware mental modelers are the ones who know this work is necessary and are actively working to advance it. These can be our DEI practitioners, human rights activists, and social justice workers, but they are also regular people who work daily to advocate for others. These individuals work to bring others to the forefront and to make space at the table to center voices that are rarely heard from.

Active awareness can be practiced by speaking up for silenced voices, self-educating through books, documentaries, discussions, etc., and pushing for equity and inclusion in personal and professional spaces. Because the actively aware are so involved, they are the key champions to bringing the passively unaware and passively aware to the party.

At times, active awareness can go a little too far and even sometimes hinder the efforts to advance one's engagement in DEI work. Those who have hyperawareness are often early adopters of the work, or they have been victimized in such a way that they are headstrong about the work and wish to see results by any means necessary. An example of overactive awareness is cancel culture. If a person/organization shares something offensive, exclusionary, or politically incorrect, this mental model will cancel the person/organization; instead of extending grace and allowing for correction, growth, and progress, these people automatically ostracize.

We are all human. We are going to make mistakes. By going to extremes when a person or organization makes a mistake, we push people further away from this space. While we need to hold people accountable to change and learn from their mistakes, we must extend grace and avoid being overactive or aggressive because aggression will only be met with aggression. When this occurs, we lose all opportunity to influence and increase the likelihood of behavior change. Sure, you want people to do the work of DEI, but do you want them to do it despite or because of?

Now that we have identified the mental models of DEI, we can recognize where we are (and where others are) in the journey and collectively work to individualize our approach to bringing people along on this journey to create a more equitable society.

Critical REFLECTION

The tools we leverage to bring people along in organizations can also be powerful as you engage with this book. I'm ending this chapter with some agreements I want you to partner with me on (as the author of this book) and partner with yourself on as you move through each page.

To achieve any lasting impact, we must have deeper conversations with ourselves and with others to strengthen understanding and awareness of these complex issues.

The undoing of societal injustice always begins at the personal level. It always begins with you.

So, I'd like you to reimagine how you're showing up to the exercise of reading and engaging with this book. Stay open to adopting a different mindset. We're weaving deep threads from the personal to the organizational, and that requires a willingness on your part to learn, to grow, and to act.

Together, we're going to reweave the fabric of a society that benefits all humanity. Trust the process, and know this vision will create a different type of space for you—one that will inspire different questions and help you define what allows you to show up as your bravest self.

Begin with an honest evaluation about which of the current DEI mental models you are currently operating from. Define the model (which is likely to change by the time you have unraveled the tangles of confusion), and adopt these following practices:

- ● **LEAVE ASSUMPTIONS AT THE DOOR.** Harmful stereotypes about certain groups can cloud your judgment. It's a good idea to check in with yourself and make sure you're not carrying any assumptions that can get in the way of having an open mind during a dialogue (whether that's with someone else or your own internal chatter).

- ● **BE YOUR AUTHENTIC SELF.** This means being honest with yourself. The most powerful realizations and fruitful outcomes happen when people show up authentically. Authenticity can make some of us feel vulnerable, but there's strength in it as well. Make sure you're not putting on a facade for yourself or for anyone else. Give yourself permission to let your guard down and acknowledge what you feel. Keep notes about what is coming up for you.

- ● **HONOR YOUR GROWTH.** You may notice you have an epiphany. This is a telltale sign you're experiencing a moment of growth. Growth can look different for everyone. For some, it's feeling the need to offer a genuine apology for a past behavior. For others, it's committing to listening first instead of speaking. Whatever that looks like, lean into the transformation.

- ● **EXPECT AND ACCEPT THAT THERE WON'T BE CLOSURE.** We're conditioned to believe in instantaneous results, but people need time to process what they've read and experienced. Give yourself space to do the internal work. Remember that this work really is like untangling knots that have kept millions of people in underrepresented populations bound since the founding of the United States of America. We are all wadded up individually and collectively in deeply complex ways. We cannot expect to understand all this right away. Keep an open mind. Withhold judgment, and become aware of any habitual responses that come up again and again. Move through each section at your own pace, and take whatever time is needed to thoughtfully and deeply reflect on how these concepts show up in your own life.

Humans are **99%** **identical.**

Inclusion recognizes that

 **All People**

are entitled to humanity and to dignity. Every voice matters. Every person contributes value.

DEI is *everyone's* Responsibility.

Race + Gender

are cultural concepts, **not** biological ones.

There is no finish line.

DEI is a **dynamic, transformational** journey.

There is **no one path** to DEI.

DEI *is* **NECESSARY for** *Survival*

 DEI work doesn't imply that white people have not had any **burdens or hardships.**

DEI IS A LOT MORE THAN *Race + Gender,*

it includes degrees of:

- *Physical Abilities*
- *Sexual Preference*
- *Economics*
- *Trauma*
- *Age*
- *And more...*

 *Remember*

- Awareness and reflection
- Be intentional
- Recognize passivity is a barrier to change
- Be open
- Follow the call-to-action
- Understand everyone has bias
- Choose courage over comfort
- Actively seek more information
- Look for the evidence

CHAPTER 2:

The Power of Story

Not everything that is faced can be changed, but
nothing can be changed until it is faced.

—JAMES BALDWIN

I was facilitating a group session one day, and there was a woman of Haitian descent in attendance. She very emotionally told the story of how, when she was in grade school, because of her accent she was not able to pronounce all the English words clearly.

One day, she stood up and asked to go to the restroom. The teacher started mocking her, saying, "I'll let you go when you can learn how to say bathroom." She was desperate and kept asking the teacher to allow her to go, but the teacher refused.

With tears in her eyes, she revealed that she ended up urinating on herself. The teacher did not see the humanity in her accent and mocked her. The kids were laughing, too, and she said, "What that did to me is, it scarred me to the point where I did everything I could to try to reverse that accent. I worked so hard."

And then she told us, "While you're hearing a little bit of it now, it is because once I healed from that, I then went back and tried to reestablish my accent."

Few things have the ability to change hearts and minds more than a powerful story.

Humans have been sharing stories with one another—about their lives, beliefs, experiences, and environments—for at least thirty thousand years.[8] Every culture on the planet has a rich history of storytelling as a primary means of creating connection, safety, and belonging.

Stories exist to help us learn, retain information, and make sense of the world around us. Chemicals such as cortisol, dopamine, and oxytocin are released in the brain when we are told stories that help us remember, keep us engaged, and help us learn how to navigate life's opportunities and challenges.

We are neurologically hardwired to pay attention to stories as a means of establishing connection with others. When someone shares a story that evokes emotional reaction, our brains literally sync with theirs, and we feel as though we are part of it. You might have experienced this before when you've gotten lost in a great film, piece of literature, or spoken word. You slip into the lives of others. You experience different worlds and events, and you feel it as if it were real, as if it were happening to you.

As I am an expert in marketing communications, wielding the power of story to create connection and systems change is a distinctive skill

---

8   Tyson Brown, "Storytelling," National Geographic Resource Library, May 20, 2022, accessed June 4, 2022, https://education.nationalgeographic.org/resource/storytelling.

set I bring to DEI. Personal stories break down barriers much faster than checklists, data, or protocols. On the most fundamental level, they communicate our biggest challenges and our deepest desires to be fully seen, accepted, and valued as we are.

We are so accustomed to operating project to project, deadline to deadline, that we may not pay attention to surroundings, have situational awareness, or even notice the experiences of our peers. If DEI efforts are to be effective, we must get proximate to others' lived experiences. We must be able to witness lives that are different from our own in order to gain knowledge and understanding.

If DEI efforts are to be effective, we must get proximate to others' lived experiences.

When I bring new groups together, one of the first things I do is have leaders, stakeholders, and team members share their DEI stories and hold conversations around what comes up.

I define storytelling as a conversation that provides a perspective, point of view, or thoughtful commentary to a group discussion. Think of it as putting yourself in a vulnerable position where you are willing to release portions of who you are, your thoughts, sentiments, and feelings, to allow others to have a deepened understanding and call to action.

A DEI story can be approached in a couple of different ways. The first way involves just being open about the intersecting identities that people may have and how that shapes their lens, how they show up, how they view the world, and how they interact. An intersecting identity can contain multiple factors that make a person unique, including their race, genetics, gender, health, economics, familial role, profession, and more. The second way is to define a turning point or impressionable moment in the participants' lives, when they really didn't realize inequities exist along with associated behaviors that cause people to feel excluded.

Sometimes just assessing how psychologically safe we may feel is a good start, letting that serve as an entry point for people to share stories, narratives, or commentary around. It could include simple questions such as the following: "Have you ever been ignored in a discussion? Have you ever been rudely interrupted in a meeting? Have you ever felt that you were a target of a negative stereotype?"

When we show up, share, and listen to one another's vulnerable, eye-opening, heartbreaking, anger-evoking, awkward, regret-filled, and enlightening DEI stories, it changes us—if we let it. We build inclusion. We build awareness. Stories are the threads that connect us to one another. They strengthen our relationships and form new pathways of belongingness.

Stories require us to get out of our bubble and to quiet our egos. They require us to slow down, get our head out of the sand, and take time to feel with people—not feel for them but feel *with* them, as Brené Brown always says.[9] And the best way to feel with people is through storytelling. People don't tell their kids facts at night. It's not "You ready for your bedtime facts?" No. It's "You ready for your bedtime story?"

Storytelling also helps move the dial toward clarity and intentionality. When you are in conversation with someone who uses feel words such as "I'm concerned" or "I'm afraid" as they speak about their lived experiences, you can't help but have some level of emotional connection to that person, to their plight. That's where empathy and compassion come in, which tend to inspire a call to action.

---

9   Brené Brown, "RSA Short: Empathy," Brenebrown.com, December 10, 2013, accessed June 4, 2022, https://brenebrown.com/videos/rsa-short-empathy/.

If we are not living in knowledge of other people's experiences, then we are often going to be unaware of the complex challenges people are experiencing. That keeps some of our most valuable people from showing up at their best and limits their opportunities for success.

When we allow story gateways to open within our hearts and within our circles, they create an appetite to do the work of inclusion. Stories help people who have been on the fence or who have lacked accountability to finally understand their responsibility. They realize they have influence in their circles and that there are things they can do at a practical, individual level.

Everyone Has a DEI Story

Everyone has a DEI story. You don't have to be a member of a historically marginalized group to have a story. Remember, diversity is a point of respect in which things differ, and that includes aspects such as age, race, gender, sexual preference, physical abilities, neurodivergence, and much more.

When we take time to learn about people's stories, they share all kinds of things. Some stories I've heard include having a child with a learning disability and the way that dimension shapes how they think about DEI. Immigrants share tales of coming to this country as outsiders and how they see the world differently. Other differences are not visible, such as someone who is a cancer survivor or a veteran, a person who is grieving the death of a loved one, or someone who struggles with daily chronic pain. All diverse. All voices that matter.

Sometimes DEI stories involve specific situations where an aha moment occurs or a light bulb goes on, even if it is unexpected, is painful, or causes grief or regret:

❁ A white woman was the only woman in a company dominated by men. She was asked to go to a cigar house or gentlemen's club after work. She said no and felt alienated because she was shunned for not hanging out with the guys.

❁ A Latin man said, "When I was a teenager, I was going to hang out at my Black friend's house, and I just kind of popped up unexpectedly because I knew where he lived. He said, 'Man, you came out here by yourself? Do you want to get shot?'"

❁ A Black man was on his way to visit a white friend when he was stopped by police. When he arrived late, his white friend said, "I can't believe that happened to you." The Black friend responded, "Well, why can't you?"

❁ A white man was part of a group in a warehouse. They were making jokes. One person's joke had a racial slur, and everyone laughed. Weeks later, this man was at a company picnic when one of his coworkers—who had been present the day of the jokes—walked in with his wife, a person of color.

When we share complex and intersectional identities that lead to inclusion, we humanize each other and practice empathy and compassion. Practicing compassion allows us to create a culture of belonging, which can only occur through genuine efforts to connect at a deeper level. All it takes to respond with compassion is an open heart and a listening ear. And when we practice compassion, we realize we are never far away from situations where we, too, may need someone's understanding, grace, or forgiveness.

Leading by example and modeling diversity offer myriad opportunities for peers, clients, and teams to learn and grow. The more we hear people talk about their lived experience, which is often deeply rooted to their culture and what they're used to, the more we are educated about their culture. That's part of shifting the narrative and creating clarity.

People can remember and relate to stories in part or in whole. We never know which aspects will resonate. Consider that the next time you wish to get a DEI point across, and celebrate each small, incremental win.

Connecting through the Narrative

Stories help us feel a greater sense of connection to others and to ourselves. Whether it's in our own spheres of influence or within our organizations, stories satisfy our senses in different ways. They allow us to witness the pain, joy, and concerns of the storyteller, which gives us greater ability to see life from their perspective. We better understand the why beyond their feelings and actions and feel inspired to provide support and encouragement. Through the act of that shared storytelling, we build cultural competencies on a personal and organizational level.

For example, let's say a colleague of mine shares a DEI story and reveals some words routinely used in the office that hurt his feelings. Later I hear a conversation between coworkers using those same descriptors, and because of his story, I'm better positioned to make comments and bring greater awareness to the situation. I become more culturally aware to shift the narrative and bring clarity to the harm that has occurred.

Stories also help us become more sensitized to hold ourselves and others accountable. However, sometimes when people are either witnesses to or victims of a poorly told joke or oppressive slurs or remarks, they may freeze in the moment because they don't know what to do. It's good to have a few tools in your toolbox for situations like these. I recommend comments that are noninvasive and that help to leave people with dignity as they reflect on the possible harm they're creating.

Try phrases such as the following:

- "Tell me more."

- "What causes you to think that way?"

- "I don't see myself in that experience."

- "Can you explain what that means to you?"

When faced with these types of offenses, it takes a whole lot of practice to be in the moment, quiet the ego, and suppress feelings and emotions. Yet when we do, this helps us respond in a way that increases the likelihood for behavioral change in the other person. That is the transformative power of story.

Whoever Is Telling the Story Owns the Narrative

Engaging the power of narrative and storytelling can be your secret weapon for success. Whoever is telling the story owns the narrative. We don't just want people to understand the constructs of diversity, equity, inclusion, and belonging, both in theory and in practice. We must also examine how we are telling the story. How are we controlling the narrative? How are we positioning this body of work with so much complexity, negativity, and even misinformation that people are holding in mind about the topic? How are we framing it?

Our perceptions of one another are often rooted in assumptions, biases, stereotypes, and misinformation. The process of collective storytelling offers real hope of unraveling the knots of political correctness, avoidance, or stonewalling and returning to the essence of our shared humanity.

We must start seeing our voice as the power to speak up and shape the story about the identities we belong to. If we don't, others will. If we get this and understand the value at a personal level, we are going to be able to take that mindset to our organizations, which are also trying to impact and transform.

Whose story do we want people to believe?

Own your narrative.

Critical REFLECTION

Now it's your turn. What is your DEI story? If you don't have a clear answer to that question yet, consider the following:

- When did you first become aware of the disparity among certain populations of people?

- When did you become awakened to the realism of racism and that white and Black people alike have very powerful stories?

If you've defined a situation, incident, event, or connection for your DEI story, write it down. Notice the words you have used. What do they mean to you? What do they say about you and your perceptions? How does this story inform where you are in the unraveling of your personal DEI journey—and, even more, where you want to go?

We are *neurologically hardwired* **for stories.**

EVERYONE has a **DEI STORY.**

We make a lot of *assumptions* about other people. **Their stories help shift our** *perspectives.*

We **must make an effort** to **get proximate** to people's **pain points.**

 PSYCHOLOGICAL SAFETY is needed to **show up, share, and listen** to one another's stories.

 STORIES *connect* **US TO ONE ANOTHER.**

Stories allow us to **WITNESS THE PAIN POINTS** of people with **DIFFERENT LIVED EXPERIENCES** than us.

Use **NONINVASIVE COMMENTS** to address **POTENTIALLY BIASED REMARKS** or perspectives.

 *Remember*

- Whoever tells the story owns the narrative.
- Examine who is controlling the narrative.
- Collective storytelling unravels the knots.
- Our voices shape the story and identities we want to belong to.
- What do you want people to know about you? About your lived experiences?
- Own your narrative.

CHAPTER 3:

DEI IS AN *Opportunity,* NOT AN *Obligation*

> We have to talk about liberating minds
> as well as liberating society.
>
> —ANGELA DAVIS

I remember doing an exercise with a client to get them to crystallize the why behind their DEI efforts. I'm a true believer that before we really start the journey, we need people to be able to confidently socialize why.

Why are you on this journey? Why is this work important to you and important to the organization? Without the why, then the how and the what get stalled. They get compromised. And so, I always like to start with the why.

We were in a room and had all these Post-it charts up on the walls. We were putting up the whys … and I noticed something. I began to put the whys on Post-it Notes in two categories. One of them contained all the reasons to do the work because of "the Obligation." And when I talk about obligation, it's where all the tactics and all the strategies are with the mindset, "How can we help out DEI? How can we help advance DEI?"

The other list included ideas that spoke to effectively fostering DEI. These were going to produce results that make us better. I labeled those "the Opportunity."

People started to notice the obligation and opportunity labels and where the patterns were going. It brought the conversation to the forefront. One of the best ways to ensure we are bringing people along and aligning in a way that can yield sustainable, positive impact is when we see this not just as obligatory work but also see the strengths of it and how it's going to make us better.

The presentation of that dialogue, the facilitation of that conversation, led to a deeper appreciation. The manager said, "I have been giving to causes that support underserved communities and highlighting particular colleagues in underrepresented populations. But my mind did not immediately go to how an opportunity mindset strengthens DEI efforts. And there is a lot to be said for that."

This realization strengthened their momentum. It certainly gave them deeper drive to see DEI not only as a business imperative but also as a moral imperative. Centering the business case as the reason for DEI places too much emphasis on capitalism rather than on humanity and thus can be harmful. When we constantly have to prove the validity of DEI work with the business case, it diminishes the human aspect of the work. The thought is, Why can't humanity be enough instead of having to justify the work with a business case? The truth is, both are critical.

We have learned that inclusion is a mindset and that harnessing the power of story connects us to one another more deeply. Stories build bridges of understanding and encourage genuine exchange. The next step on our transformational journey is to shift the way society, organizations, and individuals view DEI—from obligation to opportunity.

After the death of George Floyd and the surge of social justice movements in the United States, 96 percent of CEOs said that DEI was a top priority.[10] Yet the needle hasn't moved much in terms of efficacy and impact. One of the biggest challenges is that many organizations approach this work as a mandatory checklist of things to accomplish in a few weeks or months. That thinking limits their ability to foster true inclusion and has trickle-down effects on everything from recruitment and retention to profitability and sustainability.

To make the transformative leap from obligation to opportunity, we must unlearn the idea that inclusion is a constant struggle and an uphill battle. Doing so can minimize the frustration leaders, managers, and allies experience when attempting to do DEI work. When you find yourself asking, "What can I do to advance DEI?" recognize that is an obligation mindset. Try asking this question instead: "What can DEI do to advance my organization and society?" That's an opportunity mindset.

Obligation focuses on being a good steward in a surface-level way, whereas a DEI opportunity mindset inspires intentionality and commitment to make us better humans. That is a subtle yet incredibly important difference in energy and time investment. It helps us stay the course when things get complex and keeps us showing up and making consistent effort.

---

10   Heather McBride Leef and Benjamin Finzi, "Winter 2022 Fortune/Deloitte DEO Survey," Deloitte.com, January 4, 2022, accessed June 4, 2022, https://www2. deloitte.com/us/en/pages/chief-executive-officer/articles/ceo-survey.html.

When we learn to see difference as strength—not right, wrong, good, or bad but as opportunity—we become open to all possibilities, ask more curious questions, and listen to and share better stories. We are driven to be much more thoughtful about how to yield best outcomes and to be most effective.

Why Are People Resistant to DEI?

It goes back to individual choice. We're not going to be able to translate an opportunity mindset into the organizations we are a part of and embed that into equitable systems of decision-making and interaction if we don't adopt it on a personal level.

People can often resist DEI due to lack of exposure. There's a persistent idea that DEI is this big, audacious goal—so they sit on the sidelines. We live in a society right now where many people are afraid to even engage because they're thinking, *I'm going to mess this up*. Quite frankly, they are afraid of cancel culture.

I don't believe in cancel culture. I think it works against us. If we aren't careful, cancel culture causes us to believe that if people aren't at the place of wokeness we feel we are, then they are no longer useful to this work. I do believe in accountability and transparency. I also believe in meeting people where they are but not being content to leave them there.

How Do You Shift the Conversation?

Organizations hold two schools of thought when it comes to DEI work. The first position recognizes that people within the organization are at different learning places and believes management needs to slow walk the process to make sure everyone feels comfortable. The second stance recognizes there are a lot of people within the organization who want management to stop talking and start doing. Sometimes it's more about holding the middle by amplifying opportunities, which can only be done when obligation is out of the picture.

If we were to break down the word *obligation* into what that looks and feels like, we could say it feels burdensome. This is not a burden. People don't want to feel like a burden. They want to be celebrated and accepted. Humans have fundamental needs to be accepted, to be validated, and to have a sense of belonging. If employees are always questioning if they belong or if they are safe, they are not showing up at their best.

This is an opportunity for an organization to stand out and up for the people who work with it and for it. It's an opportunity to develop new ideas and bring voices to the table that would otherwise be silent. It's an opportunity to deliver a skillful, sensitive, and compassionate approach to leadership and business.

There's no singular approach or silver bullet. DEI needs to be built in as an ongoing strategy, an ongoing consideration.

DEI is work that belongs to all of us. To shift the conversation from obligation to opportunity, we have to be willing to help people where they are in the process and be okay with where we are as well. There's no singular approach or silver bullet. DEI needs to be built in as an ongoing strategy, an ongoing consideration. Not everybody's going to get on the boat at the same time or in the same way, and it's often very circumstantial.

People often ask me how. "How do you take someone out of a place of uncertainty, fear, lack of understanding, or the insidious 'it's not my problem' within the workplace?" As a leader in your sphere of influence, a manager, or an ally in the making, look for the opportunities that show up. It may be someone's uneducated or insensitive remark that opens the door for you to say, "I want to dig a little bit deeper to understand why that perspective exists. Let's go on this journey to get you better informed."

Like anything, the more you practice, the higher the level of cultural intelligence you build. The result is better preparation to engage in this work and a tolerance for the discomfort that arises. There's no escaping that we all are going to make mistakes. We apologize. We correct ourselves, and we move on. What represents a true apology, however, is changing the behavior.

Changing behavior is also something organizations are going to be forced to do. At the time of this writing, we've been hearing a lot about the Great Resignation, but really, it's the Great Reevaluation. The upper hand goes to the job seeker right now. They can pretty much pick their ticket and be even more demanding about their requirements. They understand that diverse threads form stronger bonds in company culture and ensure marketability in the long run.

Millennials are showing up to job interviews with a list of questions, and ranking high on that list is this: "What are you doing to help manifest a strong culture of inclusion, equity, and belonging?" For organizations that don't have a satisfactory answer, talent is moving in a different direction.

Once you know better, you do better. Organizations need to be thinking of ways to position themselves to attract and retain under-represented talent when compensation can't be the only solution. If they are not intentionally engaged in DEI, they're going to be challenged more than ever. That lack of intentionality will fail to create a culture and environment where there's a strong sense of belonging, psychological safety, and belief that full success is within reach for all. That not only makes for an unattractive workplace; it's also bad for business.

If DEI is nonexistent and not part of your value set, that's a telltale sign—not only for underrepresented, historically excluded groups but also for a lot of people who care about this work. Even for those without lived experiences of oppression, being part of an organization that values and employs people different from you makes a more interesting and enjoyable work environment. Job seekers now recognize that organizations with intentional DEI

Job seekers now recognize that organizations with intentional DEI practices have a competitive advantage.

practices have a competitive advantage. They are able to grow and thrive and compete successfully in the marketplace.

Organizations also need to be intentional in their conversations around career trajectories. Part of the challenge for underrepresented people is the lack of knowledge around opportunity or career pathing. Because they are outside dominant culture, they know they are often left behind, intentionally or unintentionally. They are now asking questions about advancement opportunities and want to know up front what career trajectories will be available to them.

Don't Be Afraid of the Data

We have covered a lot so far about the transformational mindset needed to create systems change. On a very practical, day-to-day level, a lot of compliance reasons exist to engage in DEI work because organizations must obey the law. Most want to stay connected to industry regulations and standards and maintain a certain minimum status to operate in that space. But what does that look like on a granular level?

Organizations must be willing to get the data and then not be afraid of the data. I'm talking about a deep-dive assessment to hear directly from those who are most disproportionately impacted within the organization. It's not enough to say there's an opportunity for improvement. Once you have gathered really good intel, you need to use it to become even more specific around how the organization will fully optimize DEI efforts.

GOALS OF AN ASSESSMENT

Part of getting comfortable with the idea of a deep-dive assessment is to know what it is and what it aims to accomplish.

Assessments do the following:

- Analyze the specific ways in which policies, management, leadership criteria, and culture are supporting or acting as barriers to diversity, equity, and inclusion efforts.

- Gather data on the implementation and execution of such policies to determine how effective they are and whether or not they are having the desired impact.

- Gather data on employees' perceptions of how inclusive the overall climate is.

- Gather data on the perceptions of the effectiveness of the services/programs provided by organizations relative to diversity, equity, and inclusion.

- Propose recommendations and metrics that organizations can incorporate to address the opportunities for improvement identified through the DEI assessment.

ASSESSMENT DATA COLLECTION STRATEGIES

You are also going to want to be thoughtful about identifying multiple modalities. That could include learning and development experiences, awareness opportunities and exposure, one-to-one conversations where you're influencing people's mindsets, sharing of articles, or bringing facts and data to the conversation. Among the collection strategies I employ are the following:

- **FOCUS GROUPS:** To draw upon participants' attitudes, feelings, beliefs, experiences, and reactions in a way where other methods are not applicable.

- **DEI SURVEYS:** A way to gain qualitative and quantitative information and demographic data and also generalize findings from a sample of the population.

- **ONE-ON-ONE INTERVIEWS:** Provides a safe space for employees who wish to expand on survey responses and don't feel comfortable in focus group settings.

- **LEADERSHIP INTERVIEWS:** Understanding leadership readiness and vision for DEI is crucial for strategy development and implementation.

- **CLIENT ASSETS:** Review of policies, procedures, and systems to evaluate alignment with DEI best practices.

What Does DEI Look Like in Practice?

It is about creating and really leveraging those moments when you can gain traction. From an enterprise perspective, it's looking at the business case and outlining quantifiable and qualifiable reasons why you should be thinking about DEI—for example, "hiring more women or people of color results in better financial performance." Additionally, organizations with diversity are

- twice as likely to meet or exceed financial targets,

- three times as likely to be high performing, and

- eight times as likely to achieve better business outcomes.[11]

Here are some other business-case considerations:

- Changing demographics worldwide and within America

- Increased generational mix and differences

- Ongoing war for future top talent (attract and retain top talent)

- Expectations of clients, customers, and members

- Societal and cultural shifts

- Growing multiracial and identity categories

- Complex social issues (racial inequities crisis)

- Improved productivity through increased engagement (better performance, less turnover, favorable perceptions of the organization)

- Greater innovation and creativity through encouraging diversity of thought

- Social responsibility requirements

---

11   Juliet Bourke and Bernadette Dillon, "The diversity and inclusion revolution: Eight powerful truths," Deloitte Review, Issue 22, January 2018, accessed June 4, 2022, https://www2.deloitte.com/content/dam/insights/us/articles/4209_Diversity-and-inclusion-revolution/DI_Diversity-and-inclusion-revolution.pdf.

- Community partnership investment/engagement

- Succession planning (invest now for your pipeline of future leaders)

- Think global (better global picture/context for international or cross-cultural business)

- Market opportunity (better business development opportunities in a changing marketplace)

- Mirror the marketplace (reflect your customer and your customer's customer)

Other benefits include corporate citizenship, the moral imperative, and being perceived as an organization that really cares about community and humanity.

Although we don't need to make a business case out of DEI for everyone, finance and marketing people want proof around diversity. The C-suite always cares about the bottom line. Part of being effective as a DEI practitioner, leader, and ally is to wield a different set of tools for the specific audience you are addressing. As mentioned earlier, both the business imperative and the moral imperative are necessary for transformation.

Activity versus Impact

People often confuse activity with impact, both personally and organizationally. Activity has a start and an end date. But a mindset shift is growing and ongoing. When organizations and leaders become serious about advancing the work of DEI, what feels like progress to them is often just activity in any kind of movement. It could be a singular program, initiative, or cultural event. That's not to say one-off activities can't be useful in small ways. The challenge is that it makes people delusional in thinking they're doing the work effectively. I always encourage people to be driven toward impact, which forces them to use critical-thinking skills and to become calculated and strategic. It allows them to cull from insight and intel to inform the best ways to create inclusion and build pathways toward equity.

When organizations are focused on impact, they're willing to get to the crux of the matter. They are committed to identifying the root causes of issues that could be compromising diversity, equity, and inclusion. They solve for it there. If you are in one of those organizations, that means you're going to be focused on systems change, policies, procedures, cultural aspects, the full DEI transformation—not just a singular activity.

When it's a singular activity, you're missing the accountability mechanisms. You're missing the measurement-tracking frameworks. You're missing the clarity around the prioritization of what success looks like. Driving for impact is what gets you there and all of us there together. It's a deeper, more comprehensive way of ensuring and exercising intentionality toward sustainable change.

Let's look at activity versus impact through a situation that organizations experience often—the hiring of a diverse candidate. A leader might say, "We need greater diversity," and I will respond by agreeing that it is important to think about representation. However, this is just an activity if the company does not align efforts for some type of internal cultural audit or assessment to make sure that interactions, culture, and decision-making are all facilitating opportunities for success for diverse candidates. If none of those are also in place, they're going to have a revolving door. That's the difference between activity and impact.

If we can get people to lean into DEI as an opportunity instead of an obligation, it helps build momentum and traction for the work. Excitement and expectation build, and it naturally furthers the work. Having others gravitate toward, get excited about, and engage in DEI work also creates a stronger likelihood for beneficial outcomes—the changes are realized sooner.

That part of it should never stop. There's always value in continuing to reaffirm and to deepen excitement and engagement around this work. You have people who are joining and exiting organizations and spheres of influence all the time, even from a leadership perspective. We have to see DEI as dynamic and evolving. We are creating changemakers and change agents for a more equitable society. The work never stops.

Critical REFLECTION

Think of a situation you have been in, have witnessed, or have read about where an individual or company has demonstrated a clear attitude of obligation to DEI.

What happened as a result? Who was impacted, and what was the outcome? How did that make you feel?

Now let's envision that same situation—but this time where the parties involved handled it with a mindset of opportunity. What was said or done differently? What positive outcomes may have resulted?

Chapter Three: DEI *is an Opportunity, Not an Obligation*

Obligation *focuses on being a good steward in a surface-level way.*

An **OPPORTUNITY MINDSET** *inspires* intentionality and commitment to **MAKE US BETTER HUMANS.**

See *difference* **as a** *strength.*

EVERYONE IS AT A DIFFERENT POINT IN THE DEI CONVERSATION.

Cancel culture **isn't effective in BRINGING PEOPLE ALONG.**

JOB SEEKERS HAVE THE *upper hand* **AND DEMAND DEI COMMITMENT.**

Remember

- It's not the Great Resignation—it's the Great Reevaluation.
- Companies are going to be forced to commit to DEI if they want to stay viable.
- Don't be afraid of the data.
- Develop multiple modalities, including one-on-one experiences, conversations, sharing of facts.
- Aim for impact over singular activity. Activity has a start and an end date. A mindset shift is growing and ongoing.

CHAPTER 4:

Bias Is like a Disease

My humanity is bound up in yours, for we
can only be human together.

—DESMOND TUTU

I was on location for a meeting with my employer at the time, and my supervisor had accompanied me. I had done all the preparation work, so I was prepared to present the data.

As I was presenting and sharing, the white male franchise owner stopped me. He asked a question, and because he stopped me and asked the question, I proceeded to answer.

As I did so, he said, "Wait, can you let him answer, please?" and pointed to my white male colleague.

My white male colleague said, "Well, actually, you don't want me to answer because I have not been running point on this. I am here mostly for decoration."

He was trying to make light of the situation as best he could, but what he did was actually show up as an ally in that moment. He was saying, "She's been running point on this. You need to listen to her."

For whatever reason, the client felt he couldn't hear from me as a Black woman—the Black woman seated next to a white male colleague. His perspective and bias was "I have more confidence in hearing it from him, even though the 'him' knew nothing about it."

As we continue untangling the knots that keep us bound and frayed, we must be willing to get to the root causes that compromise inclusion. Bias is among the biggest perpetrators.

Bias is like a disease: we need to stop it before it spreads.

The lens through which we see the world, and one another, is shaped by what we have learned from our families, friends, communities, media, education, and lived experiences. Psychologists call this conditioning, and it creates biases or preferences toward certain people, beliefs, and behaviors.

We all have bias. It doesn't make us bad people. It makes us human, but it also does not exonerate us from the consequences of our actions.

How does bias work, exactly? You might recall I used the analogy of how we all have a living record inside us. Any time we encounter a person different from us or a situation we are unfamiliar with, our brains unconsciously reach into that record, into those memory stores, to try to find an association. This part of our neurological processing is as ancient and primal as humans are and comes from what is referred to as "the lizard brain." Its critical function is to keep us alive by assessing, in a matter of seconds, whether we are safe or in danger.

Because this process is involuntary and instantaneous, we often end up projecting assumptions, generalities, or stereotypes onto others every day. We are often totally unconscious of the fact that we're doing it because those biases or misinformation can come from so many places—individuals, institutions, relationships, and even the influencers you follow on social media.

Reaction to this instantaneous bias is twofold. First, it makes humans react with biases and behaviors that are often inappropriate for the situation, and it creates harm to the person on the receiving end.

Second, the person projecting the bias and/or the person receiving the bias may be triggered into the stress response cycle—known as fight, flight, or freeze—when a perceived danger is detected. Stress chemicals such as cortisol and adrenaline flood the body, and blood rushes to the limbs so the body has energy to escape.

The stress response also shuts down nonessential functions such as metabolism and access to the prefrontal cortex, the brain's center for logical thinking and good decision-making. When we're in that stress mode, we literally cannot think straight. Our bodies are on overdrive, and we function only in reactivity.

Any number of things can trigger that reactivity, and when it surfaces, it literally gets into our psyche and into our mindset. It impacts our decision-making and the way we perceive others and interact with them.

We must unlearn the misinformation we have formulated about certain people, because remember, it's simply a record that has been stored, and something has triggered it. It's a habitual, unconscious reaction, not a conscious response.

This type of nervous system reaction is also contagious. When someone is deeply triggered, there is a ripple effect to all others who are in proximity—they can literally feel it—and there may be subsequent reactions that create further injury. So, knowing our biases is not just a good idea; it is critical to responsibly taking care of ourselves and others.

We must begin to address bias as something that perpetuates harm to the point in which it operates like a disease. It can eat at the body. When psychological safety is being compromised, it can cause emotional stress, and that can lead to all kinds of health issues, especially for people of color. There is strong evidence to support increased illness, physically and mentally, in historically oppressed populations that have been ongoing recipients of biased and unjust practices.[12]

Again, bias is human. Yet when we find ourselves entangled with it, we need to know how to respond so that we aren't adding salt to the wound or allowing it to spread, to fester, and to create toxicity in other parts of our bodies, personally and collectively.

Understanding and recognizing unconscious bias empowers us and everyone we meet. It can help us examine and correct our bias as it shows up, help us identify when we or someone we know has been a victim of bias, and help us gain confidence to speak out against biased behavior we witness.

Mindfulness as the First Step

Throughout this book, I've repeated the power and purpose behind intentionality in realizing inclusion in our lives and in our society. Intentionality begins with awareness, and mindfulness is how we

---

12   Ayah Nuriddin, Graham Mooney, and Alexandre I. R. White, "Reckoning with Histories of Medical Racism and Violence in the USA," *Lancet* (October 3–9, 2020): 949–951. https://www.thelancet.com/journals/lancet/article/PIIS0140-6736(20)32032-8/fulltext

become aware. Mindfulness creates the conditions in which intentionality can truly take hold and flourish.

If we are to become aware of our bias, we must cultivate mindfulness as a daily practice. Mindfulness is defined as "intentional, nonjudgmental awareness of moment-to-moment experience." The very core of mindfulness is staying awake and aware, paying attention to what is arising in the present moment. That means our thinking is not lost in the past or in the future. It is attending to what is in front of us, in real time.

Intentionality begins with awareness, and mindfulness is how we become aware.

Mindfulness practices are routinely taught in business settings to reduce stress and increase overall well-being. It helps address unconscious bias, the automatic or "knee-jerk" reactions we have without thinking, which impacts our work. When we are not mindful, we compromise our ability to be intentional. It's easy to approach a situation with an unconscious bias when we are not paying attention. Lack of awareness creates limitation that can lead to exclusion.

Exclusion results from bias and acting on misinformation about an individual or a particular group to limit their opportunities. Even as truths are revealed, earlier bias and misinformation continues to exert a powerful, often unrecognized influence on our thoughts and actions. Our brains unconsciously make decisions based on what feels safe, likeable, valuable, and competent.

We must be mindful of the ways our brains work for or against diversity and inclusion efforts. We have to manage ourselves before we manage others. Even if we are well informed on DEI practices and case studies, all that information could potentially pass through a faulty filter. We all record misinformation about people who are different than we are. Human beings regularly adopt ideas without even being aware of it. We all have habitual actions or responses that we don't think twice about.

Mindfulness helps to interrupt those automatic responses. It causes us to take inventory of our attitudes and behaviors—and those of the people we aim to influence—allowing us to better recognize, understand, and address barriers to inclusion.

The very act of examining our own minds opens the door to change in our activities, their impact, and even the way we experience our work.

Mindfulness ...

- helps ensure our efforts have a more lasting impact;

- makes it easier to be diligent and avoid becoming sidetracked by challenges to our own mindsets or those of others;

- allows us to better assess situations and structures to find the right remedies;

- helps us move from passive to active approaches, which have more impact; and

- helps us gain traction more quickly, making the work and the journey more fulfilling.

Mindfulness Practices

Mindfulness takes practice, just as diversity and inclusion work does. Here are four activities to help you get started:

1. **Present-Moment Awareness (five to ten minutes):** When you encounter someone new or familiar, listen closely to the words they say. Note their meaning and unique-

ness. Try to understand the person, pause, and avoid quick judgments and criticisms.

2. **A New Vision (five to ten minutes):** Choose a handful of small, familiar objects—a ball of yarn, a cell phone, a toothpick, an apple. Look at the objects with fresh eyes. See if you can find one new detail about each object that you didn't notice before.

3. **Focus the Breath (five to ten minutes):** Choose a quiet place and sit with your back straight but relaxed. Become aware of each breath as it moves in and out of your entire body. Anytime a thought arises, gently redirect your attention back to breathing. Simply become aware of what's happening around you.

4. **Calm the Inner Judge (twenty to thirty minutes):** Recall a strong judgment you've had about yourself or someone else in recent days. As you think about this judgment, take a few minutes to investigate how your body feels. Was it a reaction to a situation, to something, or to someone? Spend some time investigating the thoughts (whether they are opinions or facts) that come into your awareness. What emotions accompany this judgment? Fear, pride, sadness, rage? Does this judgment appear often? If so, why might you be having such a strong, automatic reaction? Does it make you feel more separated or more connected to others? Do you know where it comes from? Write down any ideas that surface.

Mindful Interactions

We can bring mindfulness and intentionality into all our interactions. I typically recommend that people begin sessions with some simple breathing exercises. I have them close their eyes and envision for a moment how they want to show up to the conversation or learning session.

This is especially helpful when dealing with someone who is very different from you, because that difference can automatically create the potential for tension points. If you know that, take a moment before you engage to ask yourself how you want to show up. Are there any long-held biases that you have a tendency toward and should be on guard against? Be mindful about your intentions, including the ultimate goal. Is it to be right? Is it to prove somebody else wrong? Is it to get a certain solution?

Most Common Biases

There are many biases that show up personally and professionally. In addition to age, race, and gender bias, some consistent biases show up in the workplace. Below, let's look at a few that routinely appear during the hiring process:

- **AFFINITY BIAS:** Gravitating to people who are like us in appearance, background, or beliefs.

  HOW TO AVOID: Take note of similarities you have and whether the person is a "fit" or an "add" to company culture.

- **CONFIRMATION BIAS:** Seeking out and interpreting new information in a way that confirms already existing beliefs.

HOW TO AVOID: Ask standardized, skills-based questions as opposed to off-the-cuff questions to provide equal opportunity to stand out.

● **APPEARANCE BIAS:** Making instant judgments based on the appearance of an individual—for example, dominant social norms of weight, height, and beauty.

HOW TO AVOID: Screen job candidates by phone.

● **NAME BIAS:** Judging a person based on their name and perceived background.

HOW TO AVOID: Omit names and personal information on job applications, and assign numbers instead.

● **ATTRIBUTION BIAS:** Assessing others' achievements as the result of luck or chance and evaluating their failures as their personality or behavior.

HOW TO AVOID: Ask clarifying questions, and don't make any assumptions.

Disrupting Unconscious Bias

I'd like to share an example of disrupting unconscious bias in the workplace. I was working with an organization and leading their DEI work, and we were in a senior team meeting. At the time, the CEO was a white male colleague, and we were talking about a women's event to advance women's leadership and corporate board service.

We were in a deep discussion about having to potentially change the date. As the event planner, I was asking, "Why would we change the date? The date's been set for a long time." Turns out it was because another meeting was also being offered by this same organization that created a scheduling conflict.

The CEO said, "I don't believe rescheduling the women's event is going to be an issue because a lot of the board members were going to be at that other event anyway. Not a whole lot of women would be impacted." And I remember I stopped him and said, "Tell me more about that."

Bottom line—he assumed he could go ahead and schedule this other meeting that involved board members because few of them were women, and they probably would not attend the event designed to help advance women in the workplace.

I explained to him we had a challenge. While this event was for advancing women's leadership, white men who often are in positions of power and privilege have the chance to help shape culture, policy, and procedure and mentor, coach, sponsor, and open doors for women. So this was not just an event for women. We needed men in the audience.

This was unconscious bias on his part. He admitted he had never thought about it in that way.

I said, "It does us no good to have an event with a whole bunch of women talking about needing to be on more boards. Meanwhile, there's not one board person, not one man in the room. What good does that do? How is that really going to help us move the needle on this? We're talking to ourselves."

Cultural Intelligence

Cultural competence—or cultural intelligence, as I like to call it—is part of the ongoing DEI transformation. We will never arrive at a point where we're completely competent around everything concerning all cultures. Yet there are ways to reduce bias and build our cultural intelligence as we're forming relationships with people who are different from us.

Choose someone in your network whom you are really in partnership with around the work of DEI. Ask that person, "What do you never again want people to say, think, or do toward your group? And what do you value that you want people to know?"

As you engage in these types of conversations, enter them willing to listen intently. Listen not to react but to learn. After you listen to learn, there is a responsibility surrounding what you do with that information and how you seize the opportunity to shift the narrative.

That is why I call it the power of building cultural intelligence. Whenever bias creeps into someone's language and they use prejudicial remarks or stereotypical sentiments around certain populations of people, you're now armed with other information. You have learned firsthand what people from that population never want you to say, think, or do as well as what they value. You can replace some of the negative information with the positive information.

Restorative versus Punitive Justice

Even if we're doing things well to try to avoid and prevent bias, it's still going to show up. We're not going to be perfect 100 percent of the time. So, when bias does create harm, it's an opportunity for people to think about what to do in that moment and to course correct.

When we have created harm, we have one or two options. Restorative justice allows us to take responsibility and try to repair the damage. Or we can react in a punitive manner and try to defend the action.

Punitive justice often expresses itself in dialogue as blame and punishment. The language is dehumanizing, adversarial, and controversial. Because we're motivated by controlling the behavior using fear, we feel like we're put on the spot. We want to shift that negative energy onto the other person rather than just seeing it in terms of bias that we all harbor.

When we are focused on restorative justice, we ask questions that focus on identifying the impacts and needs of the individual. What are the implications? What do they need? Our language shifts toward being very humanizing and collaborative because our entire motivation is to build and repair the relationship. We know that we've created harm. We don't try to justify that we intended a different outcome.

Think about the impact on the person who has been harmed. They feel isolated. They feel embarrassed. They feel unsafe. If we approach it from a restorative perspective, our mindset is focused on what we need to do to ensure that we are not creating future harm.

Some of the emotions that can result when bias has caused harm include anger and rage, frustration, mistrust, and feeling let down, drained, or disappointed. I remember after George Floyd's murder, *exhausted* was the number one word that people would use to describe how they were feeling, particularly Brown and Black people. "I'm just tired. I'm just over it." Other words included *embarrassed*, *shamed, unappreciated, unseen, vulnerable, withdrawn, overwhelmed*, and *stressed*.

I am really big on encouraging people to listen for feel words. When we hear those feel words, we have to say, "That was the impact. What are the needs of the individual?" And what they need in those moments is empathy. They need forgiveness from self, because sometimes they will blame themselves. They will pretend or assume something they did caused them to deserve that harm, and that's never the case.

Additionally, one of the needs we have is for the harm to stop. We need to not be defined by that particular situation or incident and harm. We need to have our trust rebuilt. We need safety—both emotional and physical sometimes, depending upon the circumstances. We need time and space to process and reflect.

If you're one of those individuals who rushes toward seeking forgiveness and you aren't allowing people the space and time to process, then you're creating further harm without realizing it. If someone tells you, "Just give me some time. I'll come back to you," you need to honor that.

People need validation of their feelings and their perspective. They need acceptance and belonging. They need acknowledgment of the harm. Sometimes they're simply looking for an apology, for atonement. They need reassurance, support, community, and connection.

I often share the example that if you step on my toe, I can know that you didn't mean to. You can apologize, and I can clearly know you didn't mean to cause me that harm—but my toe still hurts. Let's acknowledge that and work to repair the harm. That's what I mean by restorative justice.

Speed, the Bias Enabler

Speed can be one of the worst enablers of bias and can have lasting effects. Fast decisions can hinder equitable spaces and inclusion, both personally and professionally. We don't want to move so fast in our DEI efforts that we sacrifice sustainability and fail to implement positive outcomes.

People are reaching the realization that "I'm being overworked, and I'm no longer going to subject myself to that." That's a heavy emphasis organizations are having to navigate around right now. People often have their head in the sand. They are burned out. They're just executing and trying to meet deadlines as fast as they can. That type of mentality, practice, and behavior set doesn't always allow us to be self-aware or to pay close attention to our surroundings and to the people in our environment.

When we're committed to being mindful, we are very self-aware. We are practicing observation skills, and we're good at situational awareness because we're paying attention. When we aren't mindful, it's hard for us to notice when inclusion is being compromised, which means we're not going to feel called to action to address challenges that arise.

For example, if we aren't paying attention that our colleague has shown up physically for the last five staff meetings and didn't say a word or contribute anything, then we can't recognize there's disengagement happening that is probably connected to something else. However, if we're paying attention and we're leaning in, we have an opportunity to say, "Hey, we haven't heard your perspective. We'd love to hear your thoughts."

Times are intense, fast, and uncertain. This can cause organizations to make speedy decisions at a detriment to underserved communities. You have to take a moment and pause to think of the long-term implications on DEI.

Ask yourself this: "Am I continuing to ask strategic DEI questions at every point? Am I leveraging solid frameworks around every decision made to account for DEI implications?"

In the same way organizations think about how their industries are changing and how they need to pivot to be more relevant during this climate and evolve strategically, they should keep in mind both the benefits and the implications of speed and determine a happy medium.

Organizational Bias

Unconscious or implicit bias training has received a lot of attention in the DEI community, in the press, and within organizations as a means to directly address systemic racism. Implicit bias programs aim to reduce the nonconscious prejudices and stereotypes that automatically show up and may inadvertently affect how white Americans treat people of color. While the popularity of implicit bias programs has skyrocketed, there is limited evidence they actually work. In contrast, substantial evidence exists that bias training may create the opposite of what it intends by increasing anger and frustration in white employees and further deepening bias against marginalized groups.

We must disrupt bias by evaluating, reassessing, and reimagining processes.

It is important to remember that where we sit in an organization determines what we see. If we're operating only from a mindset of our own lived experiences, then we are out of touch with the disparities that others experience. That "out of sight, out of mind" mentality keeps us from leveraging intel and creating opportunities for those who are historically excluded and disenfranchised.

We must disrupt bias by evaluating, reassessing, and reimagining processes, because bias shows up in process as well. Where are the weak or frayed threads hiding in the skein (the organization) that look perfect from the outside but denigrate the integrity of workplace culture?

If we consider the relationship between people and process, people are the ones who implement these special protocols, systems, and habits that they ask all others to follow. Do we stop there and just try to fix the bias in a person's thinking, or do we also have them transfer some of that mindset to whom they influence and the processes they develop for others to follow?

Leaders will often tell me they have some board positions to fill and want to make sure they have a pool of diverse candidates. I usually respond by asking what their current process looks like. They often have a subset of their existing board, which we know is quite homogenous because that's why they're coming to me. The challenge is, they don't realize there's a bias in their process. It's human nature to gravitate to people who are like us.

The people they're considering for those board of director roles are likely people who live in the same communities, or whose kids go to the same school, or who attend the same place of worship. They are just creating a sea of sameness instead of intentionally creating opportunities for people who are unlike them. So, therein lies a problem.

They may point to their bylaws that contain statements automatically limiting them to certain categories of people or point out that candidates have to be at a certain level within their organization. Well, if you look across many different industries and big organizations, those who are in the upper-level C-suite roles do not necessarily look like Brown and Black people.

That's where we have to be willing to reevaluate the bylaws. Perhaps we need to open up greater opportunity for greater representation, because bias exists in all levels of process. If it's the hiring process, do we have a diverse team interviewing candidates? Do we have systems and software that ensure job postings and résumés that are filtered to avoid words that skew toward men and women?

Institutional Discrimination

Institutional discrimination and systematic lack of inclusion are big players in the conversation on DEI. Although individuals may hold biases, they are ultimately reinforced by processes and systems that are inherently exclusive. Part of fostering a more inclusive workplace is running audits and assessments of your company's cultures, processes, and systems.

By undergoing an audit, you can better understand how and why people are perpetuating exclusive and discriminatory behavior in the workplace. When you look under the hood, you're able to see the institutional causes of exclusion and discrimination and work toward solving them.

I had mentioned previously that it's important to get the data. What we do not see—because of our vantage point within the company—will ultimately impact the business's bottom line. Organizational leaders are often afraid of the data. So much so that they make their own judgments about how the data looks and what they anticipate is going to happen, and it's usually on the negative side. It causes them to not even want to collect the data.

So being afraid of the data usually has two root causes. First, leaders already perceive that the data's not going to be positive, and they don't want it to be documented in such a fashion where it amplifies the negativity. Second, if they get the data and hear information, now they're going to be responsible for doing something about it.

These are accurate assumptions, because you don't do a survey without being mindful of the need for a feedback loop. You don't ask people to lean into their vulnerabilities, to give their time, to participate in focus groups, one-on-ones, and surveys only to just get the information and sit on it. Leaders already know this to be true.

One of the biggest things I tell organizations when they start to embark upon the assessment process is this: "Before you start, just know that a lot of people are going to be eagerly awaiting the results. So, if you feel like you're going to do this and then just sit on it, let's not do it at all. Save your money, save your investment, because you owe it to those individuals to close that feedback loop and leverage the data to impact positive change."

That doesn't mean that you're expected to close the loop by saying, "We heard you, and we're going to fix everything that you said was wrong," but it does mean you need to acknowledge it and then have a plan of action. Incremental steps over time can make a tremendous difference.

Stuck on Legacy

Sometimes companies get stuck around legacy and can't move forward because of the sentiment that they've always done things a certain way. Perhaps there were only one or two colors of yarn in the company's historical fabric and they are conditioned to keep operating in that space of familiarity. DEI may be complex for that organization because of what they have been exposed to, some of which is likely misinformation. How can we reimagine that? Sometimes I will even say, "Let's take the words *diversity*, *equity*, and *inclusion* off the table if that will help your organization. Let's just talk about the effective management of human difference and the value that it brings."

Leaders should recognize all data as opportunity. It could be opportunity to reinforce the things that are working well within the organization, programmatically or operationally, or even to identify opportunities to enhance and improve upon the workplace experience. Organizations often assume that when they do an audit or assessment, they're going to be expected to implement changes overnight on things that were perceived as wrong or negative. Just remember: it's about progress, not perfection. DEI is a transformational journey from the individual to the organization. It is about making and celebrating incremental change over time, as you can. That's part of the mindset shift that will unravel the knots of DEI and make it practical, doable, and uncomplicated.

By repealing, reevaluating, and reimagining company structures, the organization will create more inclusive processes and systems that foster inclusion for years to come.

- -

Critical **REFLECTION**

Now that you know the most common forms of bias, here's a simple exercise to stop bias in its tracks. Find an example of a bias you have found in yourself. Honestly reflect on a situation where that bias appeared, who was involved, and the thoughts that were running through your mind at the time. Now use the following steps to unravel the yarn back to its starting point, to its origin:

1. When you think of the moment that bias crept into your psyche and how it impacted your decision-making or interactions with others, pause and reflect on the following:

2. Where are those thoughts coming from?

3. What's the origin, and what's the cause?

4. If you pause, you will likely discover that it's unwarranted and had no relevance to the immediate situation or similar situations.

5. Think, *How can I change this narrative? Am I going to fall prey to this and allow generalizations, stereotypes, and biases to affect my decision-making, or am I going to refute that?*

6. Then, immediately change the narrative.

Awareness, coupled with reframing the narrative, will change how you're going to speak and engage. You will be able to articulate your thoughts in a different, intentional direction rather than remaining stuck in the level of bias that surfaced. Be sure to keep track of your thoughts on these pages or in a journal so you can track your progress and stay committed.

We all have bias.

IT DOESN'T MAKE US BAD PEOPLE, but it **does not exonerate us** from the consequences of our actions.

Examine
YOUR PERSONAL BIASES *so you're* **EMPOWERED TO RESPOND** *instead of* **REACTING TO DIFFERENCES.**

Bias *is* **involuntary and** *instantaneous.*

Any number of things can trigger our reactivity.

Exclusion **results from bias and** *acting on misinformation.*

Remember

- Mindfulness is the first step.
- Be diligent, know your triggers, and avoid getting sidetracked by challenges.
- Cultivate mindfulness practices such as awareness and taming the critic.
- Pause before interactions and ask yourself how you want to show up.
- Cultivate cultural intelligence.
- Focus on restorative instead of punitive justice.
- Speed is the bias enabler.
- Organizations have bias.
- Understand systemic bias and its consequences on other populations.

CHAPTER 5:

Want to Be an Ally? Earn It.

*Don't listen to those who say you can't. Listen to
the voice inside yourself that says, "I can."*

—SHIRLEY CHISHOLM

In one of our deep-dive assessments with a client, we discovered there could be some improvements in their policies, particularly as it related to parental leave.

Most organizations have maternity leave, and now they have started shifting to "It needs to be parental leave because men want to have the bonding opportunity with kids as well."

In this particular case, though, we challenged the organization to think even further and to make sure their parental leave also accommodated those who were adoptive parents and those who were foster parents.

Months later in a follow-up meeting, a woman asked to share her perspective on the new policy. She said, "It just so happened that while we were in the midst of all this, my husband and I were working really hard to solidify plans to adopt a child. Now, I'm the beneficiary of this!"

The fact that it was so big for her, that she was able to socialize it in this setting, which was a learning setting with her peers, allowed everyone to understand how it impacted her on a personal level.

"I feel even more vested and loyal to this company," she said. And all because she felt seen, heard, and valued. She felt that her situation was worthy of centering because she had an ally who spoke up and put a policy in action that would make her family life better and her commitment to the company stronger.

Allyship is part of the DEI vernacular and has seen its share of memes, social media posts, and controversies within the last few years. While many people have good intentions, the concept of allyship is often misunderstood—beginning with why we need allies in the first place.

The historical usage of the word *ally* means someone who aligns with and supports a cause or group of people. Seems straightforward enough. However, when it comes to being an ally for marginalized populations, there's a lot more to unravel and understand before buying the T-shirt and posting a platitude online.

Before anyone can become a true ally, they must understand systems of oppression. When I think of oppression, I consider the combination of prejudice along with institutional power that then creates a system that discriminates against certain groups, whether we realize it or not.

It's the systemic, pervasive inequality that is present throughout society and benefits people with more privilege, the dominant group, while harming those with fewer privileges, which is the target group. The target groups consist of marginalized populations who have been historically disenfranchised.

Think about all the "isms": sexism, racism, heterosexism, ableism, classism, ageism. Those systems enable dominant groups to exert control over targeted groups by limiting their rights, their freedom, their access to basic resources. Resources could include healthcare, education, employment, housing, wealth building—all those things.

Allyship must be put in a context of oppression, because that's really the whole point. If you're trying to help marginalized communities overcome these systems of oppression with useful action, you must understand the history that got us here.

Performative Allyship

A lack of understanding and clarity around systems of oppression has led to a lot of performative allyship, which is when you "talk the talk" but don't "walk the walk." It engages in activity that appears to support a cause, yet its interests are rooted in gaining social capital and self-gratification.

Performative allyship usually includes an easy-to-do one-off activity. Painting a mural, tearing down a statue, or posting a black square on Instagram for Blackout Tuesday in support of Black Lives Matter, for example, is not being an effective ally. Or perhaps it's adding a statement of inclusion to your company's mission page but neglecting to create policies and practices that advance the cause. Performative allyship takes no responsibility for the community it's claiming to support. It has no follow-through. It requires no discomfort. It actually doesn't do much of anything.

Here's a question to ask yourself: "Am I really doing this activity to help others, or am I doing it to position myself or my organization in a certain light that will gain me benefit?"

True Allyship

I define *allyship* as a process—a process where we build relationships based upon trust, consistency, and accountability with the marginalized identities we seek to support and empower.

Allyship is about useful action. It's not an identity. It includes any individual who's involved in advancement of an inclusive culture through positive and intentional action. If we're a true ally, we're not just someone who believes equality, justice, dignity, and respect should be provided to all groups of people and identities. We stand in solidarity with those marginalized people through useful action.

Allyship is about being in a community with people. We must understand their lived experience, their pain points. We're collaborating as an ally because if we don't have those lived experiences, we aren't necessarily equipped for partnership.

We can't assume that we know how to support people without understanding their pain points, their lived experiences, their challenges.

How do we equip ourselves for partnership? We get proximate to the problem.

That's a step that a lot of people skip. They assume they know how to help, but it causes an adverse effect. After George Floyd's murder, so many communities were creating murals and taking down statues. Don't get me wrong—for some people, there definitely could be a sense of movement and hope through those small gestures. Where it creates frustration is when it stops there and doesn't go to a deeper level to really make a difference.

We can't assume that we know how to support people without understanding their pain points, their lived experiences, their challenges. That takes relationship building. If we aren't seeking to understand the perspective of those who are experiencing disparity, that's a clear sign the action is not for true justice. We may be able to address an immediate need, but it will feel like we're creating a handout instead of a hand up.

We can get too far ahead of ourselves without really doing the legwork to understand what the needs are, what the challenges are. True allyship demands we get out of our bubble and go to those spaces and places.

If we are doing this for the population, the person, the group that we are allying and advocating for, then why would we not seek their input? Why would we not want to understand, from their vantage point, what is really useful? We need to be willing to receive the answers by asking, "What does support look like for you in this moment?" and not just take it upon ourselves to decide what is useful. If we are positioning ourselves in solidarity, what is useful can shift depending on the circumstance.

Allyship takes work. It's not as though you can just do a one and done and then label yourself as an ally. You have to earn that. And you earn it by the people whom you're allying for, when they sense your actions are useful because you've taken the time to ask thoughtful questions and to understand their lived experiences.

Solidarity means you are being active in helping to facilitate a change. It's owning that we are connected together like strands of fiber—we are stronger when plied and entwined in purpose. I think that's the important difference between performative allyship and true allyship. I personally like to challenge people: "If you consider yourself an ally, how can you stand in solidarity for those individuals? What can you do to amplify both your internal and external work to support those marginalized voices and communities?"

One of the ways allies in the making sometimes go about gathering intel is to lean on the one or two marginalized friends, coworkers, colleagues, bosses, or acquaintances in their lives. When white people ask marginalized populations to explain or to educate them on systems of oppression, they inadvertently place an even bigger burden on those directly impacted. This can be triggering or insulting, because the white person is "needing" something from the oppressed person.

Many people of color have the emotional capital and tight-knit relationships with white friends, white colleagues, where they feel they can be leaned on and it's not going to harm them. The problem is the assumption that all of them do.

Where do we feel we have that agency to ask those types of questions? What is this relationship like? Do you talk frequently, or are you just walking up to your Black coworker whom you hardly ever speak to? Make sure you have formed a relationship and have earned trust first. Otherwise, you will be creating additional harm.

Take the initiative to educate yourself. Learn what you can. Once you've acquired some basic knowledge and you know you have built a solid relationship, you may say something like, "You know what? I watched this film. I read this book, and I attended this webinar. And I'm seeing this recurring theme, and I really don't fully understand it. It doesn't have to be today, but if you're open at some point, I'd love to have some dialogue over coffee, just to hear your perspective about it as I continue on my learning journey."

Useful Action

Being a good ally takes intention and useful action. It's not just saying you think that everyone deserves full opportunity. It is actively deciding how you will help create those opportunities and how you will strategically align your thoughts and strategies in collaboration with those you're allying with and advocating for.

If someone of a marginalized identity can say that XYZ person (or you) is an ally, they see that person has sacrificed something—whether it's using their voice, challenging the status quo, volunteering, or using their personal privilege in a public space. They truly *see* that person is an advocate.

As an ally, what you're really doing is acting *for* others to help end whatever type of oppression exists. People do that sometimes by educating others, being a voice for others, being a sponsor for others, and being a mentor for others. As an ally, you are leveraging your power, influence, and privilege to help someone else overcome hurdles or barriers that exist because of their situation or oppression (whatever that may mean in their unique circumstance).

Taking inventory of our sources of power and privilege helps us define ways we can be most impactful as allies (see the checklist in chapter 6).

When we really think about the advantages our power and privilege afford us and internalize that, we become much more powerful. It isn't powerful in a way to exert authority over others or limit resources to others. We just feel much more equipped and

Privilege doesn't make us bad people because we have it—it's an opportunity to utilize what we've been given to help others succeed as well.

inclined to leverage that power honorably in the form of opportunities that open doors for others.

This is a shift in how we typically think about privilege, which has such a negative connotation. People see privilege almost like it's *a dirty word*. Privilege doesn't make us bad people because we have it—it's an opportunity to utilize what we've been given to help others succeed as well. When we fail to acknowledge that privilege naturally exists for some more than others, that's where the challenges come in.

Speaking of leveraging power, there's this notion of the white savior, someone who is going to come in and make everything right. Yet, instead of really trying to identify opportunities that position others for success, they do the opposite. A lot of criticism exists right now around white practitioners in the DEI space who are less inclined to collaborate or to make room and space for the Black and Brown practitioners. So, there's some risk to this allyship work if you aren't collaborating with those you claim you're an ally for.

Intentional Allyship

To streamline some of these concepts, here's how to be more intentional about the work of allyship:

1. **Seek out marginalized voices and perspectives to gain better cultural intelligence**. Truly learn more about different cultures and experiences. This can lead people to take inventory of their lives and define how they can potentially change the situation for someone else.

2. **Don't just talk the work. Do the work**. Not performative allyship but *real* allyship. A step in the right direction is to simply be proactive and intentional in actively learning

about the experiences of other people's lives, especially those different from us.

3. **Confront racism/bigotry, and do it with a high level of intolerance.** True allyship is not wishy-washy. It's being clear about where you sit. So many people fear being an ally because they see it as a risk to their image and they may lose some of their supporters—but again, this is a work of solidarity.

4. **As a community or business, have a high compass for social consciousness.** A lot of organizations of influence should continue to speak out about inequities and injustices. If you are part of an organization with a large volume of high-level brands and leaders who speak out against injustice, it carries influence.

5. **Give up time and money to support organizations and nonprofits that do this work.** Organizations that have a position of financial capital and can provide for different communities should give up time and money to support those organizations and nonprofits that don't have as deep a well to do their work effectively.

6. **Be vocal, and call out inequities and poor behavior.** Research shows confronting bad behavior in the moment— whether that's responding to someone's insensitive remark or calling attention to lack of representation in the room—can make allyship more effective.

7. **Do the internal allyship work, not just the external.** Many people and brands do an "external show" of allyship work without putting in the hard internal work. Take time to

examine your internal policies and cultures to ensure they are completely supported and committed to driving out inequities. The natural intricacies of business and bureaucracy can make internal allyship and DEI trickier to implement, so strong, conscious effort is required.

Progress, Not Perfection

Effective allyship is not about always getting it right. It's about progress, not perfection. We're going to make mistakes. That's how we learn. That's how we grow.

Each one of us is in a different stage of the transformational journey, and it's impossible for us to have all the answers. Every opportunity we will get to show up as an ally is different. Every person who has been the victim of bias, racism, prejudice, and unjust treatment will need something they may or may not be able to articulate. Sometimes the only thing required is to be a listening ear, to validate what they're feeling and experiencing, and to believe their stories.

Rushing into this work can be a detriment. If we are overzealous as we embark on this journey and try to solve everything right away, we're going to feel defeated before we even take the first step. We must pace ourselves. We can't try to boil the ocean.

We need to be strategic and to prioritize. DEI does not need to be overly complex. It becomes practical and grounded when we take it step by step and know we do not have to address everything immediately. That attitude burns people out and doesn't consider the importance of change management. It can create a false sense of arrival, because again, there's no destination to this. There is no end to the work. It's an ongoing, transformational journey.

Allyship as Dialogue

We will receive many opportunities to engage in allyship in our places of work. Systems of oppression have greatly influenced the processes and procedures corporations and companies have long thrived on as well as the lack of opportunities or representation experienced by marginalized groups.

In chapter 2, we discussed the importance of storytelling. In chapter 3, we outlined how adopting a mindset of opportunity over obligation moves the work forward for everyone. As we frame DEI in terms of being an ally in the workplace, there are some specific things to keep in mind.

Dialogue is vitally important. We must create spaces and opportunities in our workplaces for people to show up bravely so they are willing to engage in dialogue. As I said earlier in this book, a lot of organizations will call a space "safe" and ask employees to lean into their vulnerabilities. That's easy to say, but just calling a space safe is not what makes it safe. We must adhere to community agreements that create the conditions necessary for marginalized groups to show up at their best in this conversation, to show up brave and be met with support for their authenticity.

As DEI practitioners, we talk about community agreements all the time in terms of "expect and accept nonclosure," or "this is a no-judgment zone." However, it's the simple things that matter most: respect, vulnerability, transparency, confidentiality. Laying that framework explicitly prepares people to feel more inclined to engage.

How Do We Equip Organizations?

People within organizations need to be equipped to host and lead safe and inclusive conversations. We need skilled and willing practitioners who ask thoughtful questions, invite all voices to participate, and value the participation from everyone in the room. It's not just about choosing people who you feel can get up and talk about the widgets or the service that the organization offers. The people who are called to lead these conversations must be prepared.

The true work resides here: How can leaders, managers, and facilitators connect with people on a level when they are vulnerable? How can the organization model what it wants the guests in the room to lean into? Part of that begins with leadership. As noted, where you sit within an organization determines your perspective.

If leaders are operating from their own lived experience, they often have no proximity to the experiences of the individuals in the organization. I'm often amazed when I do deep-dive assessments and organize focus groups with the executive leadership team. I ask them questions like "How would you describe the culture in the words of your employees?" They will respond with comments such as "We're family. We all support each other." Then, I talk to other layers of the corporation, and as I keep going down, I receive completely different responses.

That shows the level of separation that occurs between decision makers and those who are directly impacted by the work experience. There's not much bridging of the gap. The solution is relationship building. If you're in the C-suite, especially now with this distributed workforce, it's much harder. You must be even more intentional. Be accessible. Walk the hallways in the office, physically and virtually, and make a point to just show up.

Leaders within an organization have the potential to be weavers of a special kind. Like skilled artisans who discover a broken thread, they can use spinners (a form of knot repair) to mend the break and join new threads. Actions that support inclusion and modeled behavior are just like spinners. They begin to fix what is broken. No resources or talent is wasted, and the company fabric becomes stronger for everyone as a result.

True Allyship Doesn't Wait

Being an ally means your words and actions show that you will not allow that pain to pass on and that it will not happen in your presence. This is true whether you are an entry-level colleague or the founder of the company.

We're going to have to lean into some skills training to help us know how to handle oppressive remarks, whether we're a victim of or a witness to that harm. Sometimes we'll be witness to something, and we'll sit back and think, *They weren't talking to me. I'm going to mind my business and stay in my lane.* That is one approach—but remember, silence is a message as well.

So what message are we sending out in that moment, especially if we're a leader in an organization and people are watching us as we sit silently while harm is occurring? It sends a message that we condone this, that we're giving people permission to keep doing it, and that it's okay. That does not serve us well in terms of really trying to increase the likelihood for behavioral change, especially if the behavior we're trying to change is oppressive and harmful.

True ally work may require sacrifice and risk. Don't wait for permission. Just do it. If we wait because we contemplate the implications, we risk not following through. Timing is so crucial in many situations where we need to course correct quickly.

We can point to common things that are considered oppressive, like personal insults and inappropriate jokes or remarks, but there's also treating people as invisible. No one can show up at their best if they're always questioning whether they belong.

Feeling invisible in a workplace or whatever the environment is makes it hard to feel a sense of belonging. It feels very oppressive because it *is* oppressive. The same is true for lack of empathy, which is often caused because we don't have that lived experience. So, we shun or dismiss someone's experience that is different from ours, almost as though we question if it even really happened. Are they exaggerating or making it up? If we don't have empathy, then we're not going to feel called to provide support for the person.

Sometimes the word *accomplice* is used to describe the work of an ally in DEI. While *accomplice* often carries a negative connotation, the point behind leveraging it as a word in the context of *allyship* is the connection to sacrifice. Being an ally sometimes forces us to choose courage over comfort, because in those moments when we are witness to bias, we really do feel called to act. The reason a lot of people don't operate in the spirit of allyship is that they understand the risk and the sacrifice.

I know it's not always comfortable to be on the side of those who may be perceived as less valuable. But imagine how they feel. Reframe the situation, and ask, "What is that going to say about us? How are they going to begin to perceive us?" That's a real fear for some people.

If you want to be on the right side of humanity, you'll do it anyway. Let's inspire accountability with authentic ally work. If you're allying for a population of people, it's important to understand that it's all about collaboration.

A lot of times people, especially leaders, will say, "I'm committed to this work," and "I want you to hold me accountable." When I tell them what accountability looks like, when I get granular, they sometimes respond with "Oh … well, I didn't mean that. I can do this, but I can't do that."

So wherever you are in the organization, the question always goes back to this: Are you really trying to be useful and helpful? Or are you more interested in doing the bare minimum or doing what causes you to feel good versus what really is the most effective approach?

We all must ask ourselves those questions.

Critical REFLECTION

Use this exercise to reflect on what it means to be an effective ally.

Sit quietly for a few moments. Take inventory, and remember a certain incident of bias, racism, or prejudice that you've been exposed to or have heard about.

Begin to think on the following:

- How would you respond in that situation as an ally? Not as the marginalized person, but as an ally?

- What systems of oppression are at work in the scenario?

- What sources of power and privilege can you leverage as an ally?

To be an ally, you must first *understand systems of oppression.*

THINK ABOUT ALL THE "ISMS":

- *Sexism*
- *Racism*
- *Heterosexism*
- *Ableism*
- *Classism*
- *Ageism*

Get proximate to the problem.

BEING A *good ally* **TAKES INTENTION AND USEFUL ACTION.**

PERFORMATIVE ALLYSHIP *usually includes an* **easy-to-do one-off** *activity.*

True allyship is a process of **building relationships** based upon **trust, consistency, and accountability** with the **marginalized identities we** seek to support and empower.

Solidarity

means you are being active in **HELPING TO FACILITATE A CHANGE.**

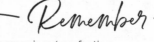

Remember

- Progress is not perfection.
- Seek out marginalized voices and perspectives to gain better cultural competence.
- Don't just talk the work. Do the work.
- Confront racism/bigotry, and do it with a high level of intolerance.
- As a community or business, have a high compass for social consciousness.
- Give up time and money to support organizations and nonprofits that do this work.
- Be vocal, and call out inequities and poor behavior.
- Do the internal allyship work, not just the external.

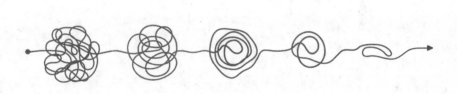

CHAPTER 6:

Understanding Privilege

Justice is what love looks like in public.

—CORNEL WEST

It took me a long time as a Black woman to even get comfortable with wearing my natural hair. I now have Sisterlocks, which are tiny locs that are going to turn into dreads at some point in time, once they mature. I felt I was not comfortable in my past at certain career points because I felt I had to assimilate. I had to show up and act like and appear as though I was one of them—them meaning the dominant culture. Members of the dominant culture have the privilege of almost never having to worry about how they wear their hair.

Once I got to a point where I was much more confident of my value and my worth—and it took a while to get there—I stopped caring as much about what others would perceive of me because I knew what I had proven.

I remember one day I started to get notes from other Black women, who would share, "I have natural hair, too, but I always wear it straight. I never thought to wear my curls. But the moment I saw you rocking your curls, I was like, 'If Nika can do it, then I can do it too.'"

And that was so liberating. It was validating. It also means I have the ability, in some small way, to influence the mindset of other women, other Black women who are watching me. When you feel validated, you know that people are watching you, and you're trying to model that type of mindset for others, you stop caring about what others think. You begin to walk confidently being who you are. But it wasn't until much later in my career that I was able to do that. Otherwise, I was masking to be accepted.

One of the most important transformational steps on the DEI journey is to recognize, acknowledge, and make a shift in the ways we perceive privilege.

When the concept of privilege is brought into the DEI conversation, it automatically creates a bit of tension in the room. Instant reactions may include defensiveness, curiosity, anxiety, anger, confusion, and more.

I define privilege as the absence of barriers and the presence of unearned advantages. Privilege can be understood as a special right, advantage, or immunity granted or available only to a particular person or group of people as given by society. Typically, this is the dominant group at the expense of members of target groups. It's necessary to understand that privilege is often invisible to people who have it.

Power often goes hand in hand with privilege. Power is the ability to control circumstances or access to resources and privileges.

Identifying your sources of power and privilege is perhaps one of the most important actions you can take, no matter where you are in the DEI process. When you can define, recognize, and then acknowledge your power and privilege, you increase your ability to act more effectively as an ally. You start to help level the playing field in terms of opportunity for all.

Sources of power and privilege come in many forms. It could be things like being a part of a dominant ethnic or racial group, or male, or being cisgender, meaning you go by the gender that was assigned to you at birth. Privilege also includes being heterosexual, not disabled, educated, or in a position of leadership within an organization, like any position of hierarchy. It's being a parent or family leader or professor or teacher or supervisor. Middle aged, and not too young or too old. All of these count.

Privilege and power are not just about race, but they are directly related to dominant culture, which we'll unpack shortly.

I often share my own personal story as a Black woman who is privileged in many regards. I grew up in a house with both parents, where we always had more than enough. I'm a well, able-bodied individual. These are things that had nothing to do with anything that I did. Those were just the cards that I was dealt.

As a person who really values diversity and has adopted a mindset of leaving no one behind, I see my power and privilege as tangible resources to help create opportunities for others.

White Privilege

In the context of DEI, we explore privilege and power through the lens of dominant culture and white privilege.

Dominant culture is one that has established its own customs, preferences, values, and norms as the standard within a society.

Nondominant culture represents all other populations who do not belong to dominant culture, including minorities and those who have been disenfranchised and marginalized and have differing cultural values and experiences. It's important to note that the term *minority* does not relate to the population of a given group but rather its cultural status.

While we've been talking about the broad definition of privilege, white privilege also exists. As stated earlier, it doesn't mean that white people have not had any burdens or hardships. It just means that the color of their skin is not the reason for those burdens or hardships.

If you are white, you are automatically a member of dominant culture in the United States, and that comes with a set of inherent privileges and power. Like all sources of privilege and power included on the list, these attributes are not earned, optional, or up for debate. They are facts that must be recognized and acknowledged to move society forward.

The reality is, it's hard for white people to face white privilege. When you are accustomed to privilege, equality feels like oppression. Privilege should not be viewed as a burden or a source of guilt but as an opportunity to make a difference, to create a more equitable world.

When privilege and power are innate to us, opening many doors of opportunity, we can unconsciously perceive and make decisions assuming that's the reality for all others. If privilege is invisible to you, that means you are not being called to action to leverage your sources of privilege as influence. You are unable to see them as opportunities to create outcomes of inclusivity, equity, and belonging for others. When you understand that's a roadblock, you've taken a huge step toward an inclusive mindset shift.

As a facilitator in this space, I'm intentional in how I utilize my privilege and power. I do a lot of speaking engagements and trainings and take each opportunity to ask event organizers questions such as "Do we have closed captioning?" If it's an in-person event, I'll ask, "What are the accessibility measures that you've put in place to make sure that people with disabilities can also participate?" So, I'm leveraging my power as a well, able-bodied individual to advocate for those I know may be challenged. That's just one example of what it might look like in practice.

It's one thing to say we need to acknowledge privilege; it's another to comprehend what is at stake when we do not.

The failure to acknowledge privilege leads to bias and oppressive behaviors because it entails a distorted viewpoint of what's necessary for success. I often hear, "I've earned all of my success. Others need to pull themselves up by the bootstraps and earn their own success." This shows a lack of clarity, a lack of understanding. Sometimes we are individuals who are given privilege in areas where a lot of others do not have those advantages.

When we acknowledge privilege, we are saying, "I want you to hold me accountable. I want to share with you some areas where I know that I am privileged." That shows your self-awareness. It gives you space, agency, and time to reflect on what you can do with that power and privilege to be an ally and to open doors for others. It ensures you don't just see the world from your lens of lived experience. It considers the wealth of opportunities that others haven't reached because of where they are within the broad spectrum of diversity and the systems of oppression they may be faced with.

Ignoring the oppression of others is a decision to tolerate inequities and exclusion. Acknowledge your privilege, and use it honorably to help someone else reach their potential.

Equity

When we talk about power and privilege, we must address equity.

Most people are familiar with the term *equality*—but that's different than equity. Equity refers to fair access, opportunity, advancement, and just practices and policies that ensure every person can thrive. Equity recognizes that barriers and disadvantages exist, that we do not all start at the same place, and commits to a process of acknowledging and correcting that imbalance. In contrast, equality implies treating everyone as if their experiences are exactly the same. These may seem like subtle differences, but they are big differences in vision and impact.

Equity is not a zero-sum game. You do not have to lose for others to succeed. Equity benefits us all.

If equality is the hoped-for end, equity is the means of getting there. Equity removes barriers to ensure people get access to the same opportunities. Social justice then aims at removing institutional, systemic, and social oppression, thereby building equity for all individuals. It is not about concessions or handouts.

An essential milestone in the work of DEI is meeting those at the table who have the wherewithal, influence, and power to create opportunities of equity for those who are historically marginalized and disenfranchised. As mentioned, equity is not a zero-sum game. You do not have to lose for others to succeed. Equity benefits us all.

People shy away from conversations about privilege, especially white privilege, because they don't understand equity. They believe they must give something up if someone else gains an opportunity. Rather, they should say, "Let's create or make a bigger pie."

Inevitably, someone will bring up affirmative action when equity enters the conversation, and this elicits an instantaneous visceral reaction. They translate it to mean they may not be in a consideration set for promotion because the company is going to have a set quota in hiring people of color. It translates to them that they're going to lose something.

As we've learned, diversity and inclusion pay dividends—in recruitment and retention of employees as well as the marketability, profitability, and competitive viability of corporations. Everyone benefits from an inclusive company culture.

If we look at how barriers and disadvantages might take shape in the workplace, some common real-world examples include women candidates with the same résumés and credentials as their male counterparts but being deemed less competent; also, candidates with white-sounding names are often twice as likely to get callbacks than those with African American–sounding names.[13]

Equity is not about the optics of age, race, and gender. Our commitment to leaving no one behind does not mean always bringing everyone to the place of full opportunity. We can align the resources all day long, but the level of responsibility is still up to the individual.

When people hear the word *equity*, sometimes they think we're saying we should give people a handout, not make them accountable, have no expectations of them, and lower the qualifications or the bar. Nothing could be further from the truth. What we are advocating is the goal that success needs to be within reach for everyone. *Leave no one behind* translates into actionable items.

---

13   Payne Lubbers, "Job Applicants with 'Black Names' Still Less Likely to Get Interviews," *Bloomberg*, US Edition, July 29, 2021, accessed June 4, 2022, https://www.bloomberg.com/news/articles/2021-07-29/job-applicants-with-black-names-still-less-likely-to-get-the-interview.

Using our power and privilege to be an effective ally and to address policies and processes within our organizations shows an ongoing commitment to equity. It ensures that everyone, regardless of identity, has opportunities for success, growth, and development.

One C-Suite Leader's Privilege

To illustrate this point, I'd like to share a story of an exchange I had with a white male executive after my company conducted a training with his organization.

He explained that he had never been interested in DEI sessions, but his organization had made them mandatory. "I came in very reluctant," he told me, "because every time I participated in these types of sessions, I have been made to feel guilted, shamed, and blamed." Then he said, "You didn't do any of that. You brought factual truth and perspective that I could appreciate, and it helped me open up and not be so closed minded."

He started sharing personal stories of how the DEI conversation had always been about race for him, Black and white, which had always turned him off. That changed for him, however, after our session on privilege. He found it eye opening to think about how we all are privileged in many regards if we were to take inventory of our lives.

He went through the exercise of defining sources of power and privilege just as you will do later in this chapter. He acknowledged he is in an executive position. He speaks the dominant language. He is cisgender.

He never thought about any of those because his point of reference was this: "I know that I'm a white man, but I grew up poor. I didn't know where my next meal was going to come from. That motivated me to have great drive to change the outcome for my kids, and so I don't like being called privileged. I feel like I earned what I have." Then he said, "But I understand now that while I may not have been privileged from a financial standpoint, I was privileged because the color of my skin is white, and I have a certain amount of power because of that."

It's as if the light bulbs went off for this leader. We didn't necessarily solve anything significant, and yet a transformation had taken place.

This is the work. This is what we want to see happen.

He walked in with his arms crossed, agreeing to listen because otherwise he might have lost his job. He walked out saying, "I look forward to the next session."

That is a win. Small, incremental steps make a difference. We're after progress, not perfection, because this is complex work. We must celebrate those small wins, those small milestones.

Masking in the Workplace

As we've discovered, privilege and power look different depending on where you're sitting in the organization and because of the circumstances that make you who you are.

Dominant culture dictates what the accepted norms are in society and in our workplaces.

Members of nondominant cultures or marginalized communities who do not carry privilege often "mask" at work. At its simplest definition, masking occurs when people disguise who they are.

It's the practice of feeling as though they can't show up fully as themselves, personally or professionally. They tone down or mute a disfavored identity to fit into an organization and conform to the mainstream.

Through a diversity and inclusion lens, masking causes people to conform to dominant thinking and shrink back portions of their identity. They end up covering what they're really thinking and feeling as a way of coping and gaining acceptance. Masking causes people to diminish portions of who they are, which is harmful and exhausting.

The Deloitte University Leadership Center for Inclusion report *Uncovering Talent* reveals that 61 percent of all employees "cover" their identities in some way—not necessarily hiding something but downplaying it for fear of drawing unwanted attention or making others uncomfortable.[14]

Masking is equally detrimental to the benefits that DEI work brings to an organization. If people aren't bringing their full selves to work and do not feel safe to disagree or have a different perspective, this does harm to the individual and the organization. It occurs most often in marginalized, oppressed, and disenfranchised populations. It is a symptom of their psychological safety being compromised. It's a form of masking, and quite simply, it denies their individuality and authenticity.

We must support productive environments and mindsets where people can "unmask" and show up as their true selves. When we show up fully, we are more productive and more authentic, and business has the potential to improve.

To prevent the need to cover or mask, we must create spaces where people feel a sense of acceptance as whole individuals, not just in certain parts of their identity. This safe and welcoming culture is

---

14   Terri Cooper, *Inclusion Survey: Uncovering Talent*, Deloitte.com, June 1, 2022, accessed June 4, 2022, https://www2.deloitte.com/us/en/pages/about-deloitte/articles/covering-in-the-workplace.html.

accomplished when stakeholders own their privilege and place a high value on uniqueness and belonging.

Don't just tolerate people showing up authentically and unmasked. *Encourage it.*

There are many ways to utilize power and privilege so that no one feels they have to mask or conform in order to thrive.

Here are some proven steps to weave a new inclusive culture that can stand wear and tear and remain in integrity:

1. **Be very intentional about creating and encouraging a culture that finds healthy conflict to be normal.**

   This is vital. We must welcome differences of opinion and open dialogue. Encouraging this level of banter produces greater problem solving, a higher level of creativity, and greater innovation and—eventually—leads to more competitive advantage.

   Create a culture that not only welcomes this type of conversation but also encourages disagreement and healthy conflict. This is not something that can passively be done; it must be integrated into leadership, general communication, standards, and company culture.

2. **Once you create more diversity, you must manage diversity.**

   It's a tough pill to swallow, but diversity by itself doesn't necessarily bring results. It's the effective management of that diversity that creates change. This is why we pair it with the concepts of inclusion and equity.

   One standout diversity and inclusion leader I often quote is Kenji Yoshino, the Chief Justice Earl Warren Professor of Constitutional Law at NYU School of Law. Kenji is frequently quoted regarding masking from his book *Covering: The Hidden Assault on Our Civil Rights.*[15]

In one famous study, Kenji surveyed three thousand employees across ten industries. Each organization had a stated commitment to inclusion, yet the survey results showed the following:

- 61 percent of the survey participants said they had faced overt or implicit pressure to cover in some way or to downplay their differences from the mainstream.

- 66 percent of employees said this significantly undermined their sense of self.

- 57 percent avoided sticking up for their identity group.

- 50 percent stated it diminished their sense of commitment.

- 40 percent refrained from behavior commonly associated with a given identity.

- 29 percent altered their attire, grooming, or mannerisms to make their identity less obvious.

- 18 percent limited contact with members of a group they belong to.

These statistics came from organizations who have a specific statement dedicated to diversity and inclusion. From their vantage point, they're putting procedures into practice and being systematic about infiltrating all aspects of the organiza-

---

15   Kenji Yoshino, *Covering: The Hidden Assault on Our Civil Rights* (New York City: Random House, 2006), http://kenjiyoshino.com/KY/covering/.

tion. Yet we still see over 50 percent of people having these experiences feeling implicit pressure to cover or mask. That's why some people say diversity can work against you if it's not effectively managed.

If people feel they have to mask because their levels of uniqueness and authenticity are not being effectively managed, they become less committed to organizations. It causes them to undermine their sense of self. So, what has to happen? These businesses and organizations, staffed by those who have power and privilege, need to create systems for learning and development. They must build systems with the goal of improving cultural intelligence and managing diversity for successful outcomes.

3. Give people full liberty to disagree both with each other and leadership.

Allow employees to be vocal with leadership. This is understandably hard for people to do and takes some training, coaching, and a culture that values speaking up. It also takes coaching of those who are in senior levels of influence. Sometimes people don't come forth because they fear the risk of retaliation. Or they fear how they may be treated if they fully show up in a capacity that aligns with their identity. Working with a diversity and inclusion specialist or coach can be extremely beneficial in helping leaders, teams, and employees to better foster this open communication.

4. **Shout it out from the rooftops—be vocal everywhere.**

Along with being vocal to leadership, people should be vocal everywhere: at work, at home, to friends, throughout their daily life. We must normalize people being their most authentic selves in society.

A simple example I like to give (and I am actively vocal about) is African American or ethnic hair. Women of color often go through long, expensive, and complicated processes to make their hair look unlike the way it grows naturally out of their head! This may sound simple or trite, but it's vital to a person's authentic and God-given identity. If we don't feel comfortable enough showing up as our natural selves (and we have to spend extra time and money to change it), how can we truly be a diverse, inclusive, and equitable society? How can we foster diverse and inclusive workplaces? People should be empowered to feel natural and comfortable. That authenticity will ripple into their productivity and engagement within the workplace.

5. **Create a feeling of belongingness.**

Place a high emphasis on authenticity and the sense of belongingness. Create a culture of acceptance. If you have a leader who is high in belongingness and who also has a high value of authenticity, then you usually have an environment that is very inclusive. This means individuals are treated as insiders but also allowed, encouraged, and welcomed to maintain a level of authenticity in that work group.

What does exclusion look like? When people in an organization are not treated as insiders with unique value. When they are viewed as the "other" or the "lesser than." If the people on the outside view other employees or specific groups of employees as the insiders, then an issue exists that needs to be resolved.

What does inclusion look like? Insiders of all types are welcomed and expected to keep a high level of authenticity.

6. **Mindfulness in the workplace.**

Mindfulness is a word that's used in so many ways these days, but as explored earlier, I believe in its importance. The bottom line is, if you can't manage yourself, you can't manage and lead others.

Mindfulness is important for leaders and those writing the reports on DEI. It's important that we are thoughtful about situational awareness. If we are mindful, we have a greater propensity toward self-awareness to observe what's happening and what's not happening. We are being more intentional and notice where inclusion can be compromised, and that's important because it gives us the opportunity to potentially change the outcome.

Being a mindful individual means you practice intentional inclusion consistently. It's easy to approach a situation with unconscious bias—operating from a place of "not being aware." Lack of awareness leads to limited thinking, limited thinking leads to exclusion, and that can lead to people leaving an organization or having to mask to survive in that environment. It's a domino effect.

We can move in the right direction if we're more mindful and create cultures of positive momentum toward authenticity.

Intellect over Emotion

Encouraging authenticity may be frightening or daunting for leaders, allies, and anyone just arriving to the DEI table. It can also be frustrating for those who are already advanced in the conversation and who want to push people along instead of inviting them to join.

This journey requires intentionality, action, and a healthy dose of patience from all involved.

It may not be a popular belief, but sometimes we must quiet our egos and emotions and lead with intellect. There would be no point (and frankly no jobs) in the DEI world if we expected people to "get it" right out of the gate. If that means the entryway into the conversation is allowing people to *not be* at a place where we'd ideally like them to be ... we must extend grace.

As DEI practitioners, we can't come across as expecting people just to get this immediately. People have been conditioned to operate as they are, to think with their level of awareness and consciousness, and they've created habitual patterns they often cannot see beyond. Our job is to support and create the shift in their mindset and actions.

Do we attack or denigrate them? Or do we find ways to engage them and build trust—and use that trust to help shift the world? Navigating this concept is difficult.

Some people will think I'm not being true to the work, and others will agree with me. But we can't just go around throwing anger, aggression, or extreme judgment at people. If people feel attacked, they're not going to engage, and nothing changes. Some practitioners have a more aggressive approach, but I think that likely diminishes the entire effort.

Bottom line—if we react too emotionally when doing this intense work, with our outcomes tied to business data and to results, it can hamper our ultimate goal of equity in exchange for reactivity in the moment.

- -

Critical REFLECTION

Take a few minutes right now, and check the privilege and power you carry.

Sources of privilege and power include the following:

- ☐ Part of the dominant ethnic and/or racial group
- ☐ Male
- ☐ Cisgender (your gender is the same as that assigned to you at birth)
- ☐ Straight
- ☐ Not disabled
- ☐ Speak the dominant language
- ☐ Neither "too young" nor "too old"
- ☐ Certain height/size/shape
- ☐ Not a mother
- ☐ Not a caregiver
- ☐ From an upper- or middle-class family
- ☐ Educated
- ☐ Technically experienced
- ☐ Wealthy (compared to peers)

- ☐ Management position

- ☐ Professor/teacher, supervisor, etc.

- ☐ Parent or family leader

- ☐ Any position of hierarchy

- ☐ Widely recognized as an expert

- ☐ Large audience (social media following, fans, etc.)

- ☐ Access to media (reporters, TV, editors, etc.)

- ☐ Respected by powerful and influential people

This list may surprise some people because it's not in the context of just white and Black—where most people's minds usually go. That's part of the transformational mind shift that makes this journey of unraveling so valuable—truly seeing the landscape as it is.

Privilege *is the absence of barriers and the presence of* **UNEARNED ADVANTAGES.**

Power **often goes hand in hand with** *privilege.*

Sources of **POWER AND PRIVILEGE** include being part of **dominant ethnic or racial groups, being male, being cisgender.**

Equity refers to **fair access, opportunity, advancement, and just practices and policies that ensure every person can thrive.**

KNOW YOUR SOURCES OF POWER AND PRIVILEGE.

Acknowledging **POWER AND PRIVILEGE** allows you to **EMPOWER OTHERS.**

If you are a member of dominant culture, you have white privilege.

Failure to acknowledge privilege leads to bias and oppressive behaviors.

Remember

- Masking occurs when people disguise who they are.
- We must create spaces where people feel a sense of acceptance as whole individuals.
- Create a culture that finds healthy conflict to be normal.
- Once you create more diversity, you must manage diversity.
- Give people full liberty to disagree both with each other and with leadership.
- Shout it out from the rooftops—be vocal everywhere.
- Create a feeling of belongingness.
- Be mindful in the workplace.
- Use intellect over emotion.

CHAPTER 7

Transform Your Culture

There must exist a paradigm, a practical model for social change, that includes an understanding of ways to transform consciousness that are linked to efforts to transform structures.

—BELL HOOKS

I was at an event where we'd assembled several different minority business leaders. These were minority entrepreneurs across the state of South Carolina, and it was so inspiring. Most of the individuals were part of cohorts for that calendar year, but there were also a handful of alumni of the program.

We were doing our round-robin of introductions, and everybody was giving their elevator speeches. We got to the point where we had probably allowed half the alumni, the graduates, to give their elevator speech and to introduce themselves, but we were running long.

To catch up, the facilitator of the meeting said, "I'll tell you what we're going to do. We're going to ask that graduates do not share so that we can get through the current cohort."

We got toward the end, and all the new cohorts had been intro-duced when one of the alumni raised her hand. She started her prompt with "I was told to always ask, so I'm just going to ask. Can the alumni that did not get a chance to go at least be given fifteen, twenty seconds to introduce ourselves?" (The current cohort had been given sixty seconds.)

The facilitator hesitated. I jumped up and said, "I really advocate for that because these individuals are here for the full experi-ence, not just as observers. I want them to have the value of being acknowledged, of knowing who's in the room, and for others to know they're in the room."

They couldn't ignore it, and the approval was given. Everybody received the opportunity to introduce themselves. Afterward, this young woman said, "My mentor told me to speak up and always ask." And it changed things. It created an opportunity that allowed some satisfaction for those individuals who were likely feeling excluded.

As we make the transformative journey from individual spheres of influence to professional places of work, we arrive at a traditionally huge tangle of dominant voices, differing opinions, and unparalleled opportunity: transforming company culture.

One misstep I've seen organizations make over and over, however, is trying to solve for DEI with programming and initiatives. Those activities can be useful, but we need to adopt a mindset of moving from activity to impact and using a deeper lens on DEI and, therefore, on the culture. The culture is all about the people. How are we bringing people in and acclimating them to our value set of DEI within the organization? That's what will build and help maintain an inclusive culture.

The first step is getting clear on the terms. I offered some level-setting definitions of DEI at the beginning of the book, but it's important for any organization to first spend some time talking about what DEI means to them—to the individuals, to leadership, and to the organization as a whole.

People have different definitions of diversity, and every organization must define it for themselves. A lot of times, people are very narrow-mindedly thinking about diversity as race, age, and gender, and it's so much broader than just the optics.

We have to take time to define terms out of the gate so that everyone understands what those words mean in the context of the organization. All employees within the organization must be able to articulate their own DEI definitions and their stories in a safe space with colleagues, with teammates, and with leadership.

What lens do you show up with for DEI? What are your intersecting identities that inform your perspectives? We often learn we've been making assumptions we weren't even aware of.

Setting Expectations

What does setting expectations look like from a DEI perspective? First and foremost, it begins with awareness along with the understanding that any learning and development experiences are continual, not just a one and done. People are continually learning and unlearning and relearning. It's not just about transferring information; it's asking, "How do we now incorporate tools and best practices that hold people accountable? How do we take our learning experiences and then actualize that learning into the day-to-day?"

Communication Strategy

Remember the assessments I spoke of earlier? Part of inclusive leadership is to make sure everyone understands the next phase of the DEI journey, including the purpose and follow-through of DEI assessments.

It's important to craft a sound communication strategy that can continue efforts to ensure momentum. If the effort is not appropriately or broadly communicated, the initiatives designed to elevate the work to the next level can be compromised. A clear communication strategy establishes trust, confidentiality, and clarity on the DEI path forward.

The communication strategy aims to educate and reinforce the firm's business case for DEI and establish transparency around the process, including intended outcomes. The assessments (mentioned earlier) should be communicated as an evolution of the process that has already been started with the firm's DEI leadership.

To ensure a good response for assessment activities, the following communication tactics should be implemented:

- ❀ Prep your most senior leader to be the voice behind the communications to establish the significance of the effort—this sets the tone and models behavior that can influence support for the work. This should include verbal announcements and initial email communications that should come from this person appealing for participation with a personal commitment to be directly involved.

- ❀ Overcommunicate the why, which is the business case for why the firm is committed to DEI. This is where you will want to reiterate the company's vision and mission for DEI. It's easier to tell a coherent story if your company has a clear understanding of why enhancing DEI is important as well as the steps it will take to ensure greater diversity, equity, and inclusion.

- Ensure leadership's plans to commit their time to participate in the assessment process (including survey and focus groups) as a model of the behavior.

- Remind staff of milestones that have already been achieved relevant to DEI goals and objectives to demonstrate how intentional planning can yield positive results.

- Highlight that this process is a journey, admitting that the company doesn't have all the answers, but that the goal is to evolve the strategy for greater outcomes. The data collected from the assessment will be catalytic.

- Set a goal for a response rate, and consider offering an incentive, like a drawing for a gift card for all focus group/survey/training participants and if your company reaches an X percent survey response rate.

- Leverage your managers/directors to make special appeals for focus group participation, and remind staff of the survey leading up to the deadline.

- Request that directors/managers/supervisors encourage direct reports to participate in focus groups/surveys. This could be a simple email directly to those immediately on their team.

- Leverage several communication channels as reminders to keep the opportunity top of mind (i.e., staff meetings, emails, a CEO video, an internal blog written by the leader, etc.). With this communication, incorporate DEI quotes and statements that reinforce the importance of the work.

🌑 Source and share articles and white papers on DEI with staff to keep DEI top of mind, which will serve as a reminder of the process underway.

Diversity of Thought

Part of helping people feel a strong sense of ability and agency within an organization is to commit to valuing diversity of thought. What does that look like in a practical way? You are very communicative about accepting, welcoming, and expecting ideas and opinions from all layers of the organization regardless of title, tenure, or position. You are mindful to center as many voices as possible.

> **The greatest gift you can give another person is to simply include them.**

The greatest gift you can give another person is to simply include them. While this sounds like a simple concept, it's rarely given full attention in our workplaces. As dominant culture sets the tone, it's easy to follow the status quo and just do the minimum, which reinforces conformist culture.

A conformist culture causes us to exclude new ideas and miss out on opportunities to innovate in systems, processes, and new product/service offerings. It shuts down voices before they even have the chance to contribute. Bottom line—inclusive environments become possible when you foster a culture of speaking up.

Foster a Culture of Speaking Up

Earlier in the book, we spoke about the importance of storytelling. Once people share their own DEI stories within the organization, it provides so much connection and clarity and bridges the divide that can exist consciously and unconsciously, preventing us from moving forward.

Changing company culture must include getting proximate to employees and listening to what's showing up from their perspectives. Moving from a conformist culture to an inclusive one takes commitment. It means intentionally and actively honoring all voices and ensuring everyone feels safe to express themselves.

Getting people to speak up within an organization is not as clear cut as we'd like to imagine. It does not have to be complex, but we must define and get rid of the barriers that keep all voices from entering the conversation. We must clear the path for inclusive communication.

Tangled Knots That Prevent Speaking Up

The number one reason people don't speak up within an organization is a lack of psychological safety. Here are some typical comments I've heard:

- "I feel like there's going to be repercussions."

- "I already feel like I'm not seen as an equal."

- "If I say something that lands on someone in a way that I didn't intend, I'm going to get in trouble."

⦿ "I'm going to be gaslit."

Gaslighting at work happens when a colleague or boss manipulates a person to the point where they question their own memory or perceptions.

Psychological Safety

According to Harvard's Dr. Amy Edmondson, psychological safety is a shared belief that the team is safe for interpersonal risk taking.[16] She points out that it isn't about being nice. "It's about giving candid feedback, openly admitting mistakes, and learning from each other."

How do we create psychological safety? We create environments where everyone's voice matters. Where we make sure people don't feel punished for their mistakes and where they feel supported through the growth of falling forward.

Sometimes people will sense that psychological safety is coddling and trying to be overprotective, but it does not mean an absence of accountability. True DEI work is not about giving anyone an excuse for skipping responsibility. It's a disservice to people if we coddle them instead of empowering them to contribute to positive change.

Encourage differences of opinion, and watch the true magic of belonging and inclusion happen. Establish and emphasize a culture of speaking up, stress the value diversity of thought offers, and encourage employees to challenge the status quo courageously but respectfully. Consider this: Do you have a culture in which people can exercise constructive candor?

---

16   Amy Edmondson, "Psychological Safety and Learning Behavior in Work Teams," *Administrative Science Quarterly* Vol. 44, No. 2 (June, 1999): 350–383, https://journals.sagepub.com/doi/10.2307/2666999.

This is where it's essential for leadership to have a great sense of responsibility and ownership of modeling inclusive behaviors, because it starts at the top. Professionals from historically marginalized communities have a greater propensity to be reluctant to speak up in these environments because they feel they have to conform instead of being their authentic selves. They are keenly aware of the differences that exist among people that look like them versus a dominant culture. Leadership can be the critical factor that shifts this employee dynamic from one of closing down to one of starting to open up to possibility.

Dialogue Is an Asset

Dialogue is one of the greatest assets we have, and we must use it responsibly. Always center as many voices as you can.

True dialogue is not a monologue. Examine how much time leadership takes in delivering their message. What's the ratio between dominant voices to underrepresented voices? If there are long periods of the same dominant voices speaking, the group tends to check out because they are not being engaged. If leadership or dominant voices always speak in statements with few or no questions, that's another red flag signaling exclusion.

We're often petrified of saying too much or saying it wrong. During times when your voice matters the most, the only wrong thing you can say is nothing at all. Dialogue that encourages everyone to speak up is essential to leveraging inclusion and belonging within a workforce. Open your mind and leverage curiosity to allow the most authentic conversations to occur.

Freedom to Unmask

The ability to fully step into the dialogue can only occur if people feel like they don't have to mask. You might recall that masking occurs when someone believes they have to cover up or hide aspects of who they are to avoid bringing attention to their uniqueness or to fit into the dominant culture's norms.

Part of transforming culture also means creating opportunities for people to know they can take up space. As a lot of historically marginalized populations express it, "I can't take up space. I have to shrink back," and that means being quiet, not speaking up. This spills over into so many other aspects of how they show up as well, such as, "Can I wear my natural hair to work? Can I speak with a confident tone without people perceiving that I am militant and overly aggressive? Can I publicly take credit for an idea?" These are a lot of things white people have natural agency over. We must understand and acknowledge that the rules have not been the same for everyone and course correct. Employees who have been used to concealing or shrinking back must see evidence they are valued, seen, and heard.

Part of the equation comes from the inside out for Black, Indigenous, and People of Color (BIPOC) individuals. A healthy ego is necessary in order to show up fully and stand in one's voice and power. That's why I often say that a healthy ego is a hidden superpower for BIPOC populations in the workplace. It builds agency in action. It allows them to know their worth. It helps them see themselves in a positive light.

This reminds me of a personal story I'd like to share. In my career, I was noticing that my white male counterparts seemed to get opportunities of upward mobility much faster than I did. I began to respectfully challenge and question so that I could understand what the separators were. I wanted to track my career pathing and career trajectory and to know why. I was getting really good performance reviews, and it just felt inequitable in terms of how promotions and leadership opportunity decisions were being made.

I remember one of the things someone said to me was "You are too ambitious. You need to be more patient." I wondered to myself if they were saying the same thing to my white male counterparts or to others who didn't look like me and who benefited from dominant culture.

I was astutely and thoughtfully just trying to understand. I wanted to know how I could meet the expectations of what they defined as success in that environment so I could also be placed on that trajectory. I let them know what I was seeing and what the disconnect was for me.

Ego is a hidden superpower, because I was very ambitious and it was part of survival for me. It was the mindset that I needed to have in an environment where I was one of the first few and only. The leadership made it seem like I was always asking for more, for more, for more, but what they didn't realize, because they were part of the dominant culture and environment, is that they didn't (and still don't) have to do this to the level in which I did along with other Brown and Black colleagues.

I bring this up because we must have a healthy ego if we want to feel a sense of agency around speaking up. Ego is not always bad. Sometimes ego is the very quality that helps marginalized communities and populations tap into self-esteem and self-importance. It enables them to feel that "Yes, my voice does count. Yes, I should have the ability to express my opinion even if it's different from others'."

A healthy ego can be used as a tool of empowerment for marginalized people instead of as a weapon for power and control.

Overcommunicate with Empathy and Compassion

There's no denying that empathy and compassion are vital to inclusive company culture.

Anytime we find ourselves in a period of uncertainty, we need to overcommunicate. We must ensure that leaders and messengers on behalf of the company are thoughtful and considerate.

There's value in leaders demonstrating vulnerability and sharing how they're navigating and being impacted by complex social issues. This allows others to know that they're not alone and that moments of uncertainty abound. Lead with a voice of authenticity, transparency, and truth. Honest updates are helpful and comforting in these times of uncertainty.

Organizational leaders should think through and ask these questions:

- Which different groups will be impacted by this decision, and how?

- Is there a way to create more equitable divisions of the impact?

- Are we communicating any changes or shifts in an empathic and inclusive way?

- Are we asking strategic DEI questions at every point and encouraging other leaders to do the same?

- Are we setting clear expectations for people to know when, where, and how we're planning to communicate updates?

- Are we communicating with encouragement and helping with morale and connection?

People need to understand that DEI transformation requires this deep level of commitment. It requires us to tease out the knots that bind us to unsustainable practices in the workplace. We have to get to the main crux of the matter. Together, we all must unravel those layers to identify the root causes of issues that are compromising inclusion.

Exercise: Community Agreements

Next time you're gearing up to have a company-wide DEI conversation, encourage leadership to take ten or fifteen minutes ahead of the meeting to name community agreements. This list is not exhaustive. You can certainly include other agreements suggested by participants. These seven are merely stepping-stones for you and your team to build on.

Community agreements are not the only solution to having powerful DEI conversations. Ensuring that you have the right atmosphere, that the timing of the meeting is on point, and that people are mentally prepared for a conversation are also important aspects. As you progress with agreements in mind, DEI conversations will become more productive and effective over time.

1. **LEAVE ASSUMPTIONS AT THE DOOR:** Harmful stereotypes and preconceived ideas about certain groups can cloud our judgment. Check in, and make sure you're not carrying any assumptions that can get in the way of having an open mind during a dialogue.

2. **NAME WHAT YOU NEED IN ORDER TO FEEL SAFE:** In DEI circles, we often say, "This is a safe space," but the reality is, calling a space safe doesn't make it true. Most people aren't mind readers. It's important for all participants

to name what they need to make them feel safe up front so others in the room can honor and respect it. Assuming everyone feels safe in a conversation is a pitfall that should be avoided. It's a good idea to have someone tasked with checking in with participants to make sure their needs for safety are being met throughout the session. This allows them to feel brave enough to contribute in a meaningful way.

3. **BE YOUR AUTHENTIC SELF:** The most constructive conversations are the ones where people show up authentically. Authenticity can make us feel vulnerable, but there's power in it as well. Making sure people know they don't have to put on a facade to be present is important to creating a safer space. It's essential to give people in the room permission to let their guards down and share their unique wisdom and perspectives with the group. When more people show up authentically in DEI conversations, more opportunities for learning and connection arise.

4. **ENSURE NO TOPIC IS OFF THE TABLE:** Part of having powerful DEI conversations is allowing topics and tangents to come up naturally. It's okay to keep the dialogue focused on one particular issue, but if related thoughts, anecdotes, experiences, and questions come up, it's important to acknowledge them. These discussions are designed to allow people to express their thoughts and ideas without judgment. Placing limitations on which topics can be discussed can stifle the conversation and leave some feeling unheard or unacknowledged.

5. **HONOR THE GROWTH:** In these conversations, you may notice that you or someone else in the room has an

epiphany. This is an indication that they are experiencing a moment of growth. Perhaps the thread of belonging just got stronger when they realized we're all in this together. Growth can look different for everyone. Maybe it's speaking up for a colleague who has been targeted. Perhaps it's acknowledging a biased phrase that was used out of ignorance and asking to be held accountable. Whatever that looks like, lean into the transformation. Think about how the conversation could be evolving the perspectives and development of other people in the room.

6. **EXPRESS GRATITUDE:** Being present and vulnerable in DEI conversations isn't always easy. That's why expressing gratitude and commending your colleagues is so important as a way to encourage participation. A good way to show gratitude is to give affirmations. That can look like saying thank you to the person sharing or nodding your head in agreement when something resonates with you. Leaning into acknowledging others encourages them to continue to share and therefore makes the conversation that much richer and more meaningful.

7. **EXPECT AND ACCEPT THAT THERE WON'T BE CLOSURE:** We're conditioned in the business world to expect to-do lists, objectives, and solid takeaways after meetings are held. In DEI conversations, that's not always the case. Sometimes when the conversation ends, people need time to process what they've heard and experienced. Practice giving people space to do the work they need to after the dialogue. Don't expect people to have action steps right away. This community agreement allows those who participated

in the conversation to process the information on their own time and come back later with more meaningful reflections.

Strengthen the Muscle of Speaking Up

Let's get granular about the real-world applications of what we've just learned:

- **USE THE COMMUNITY AGREEMENTS:** This grounds the entire organization around "Here's how we are committing to enter into these discussions." It's important to establish the safety of people at the beginning so they feel free to be transparent, to lean into their vulnerabilities, and to ask questions without being judged. They shouldn't worry whether they put all the right words together to ask the question. It is a bit of a risk for everyone involved, but it is necessary.

- **BE OKAY WITH MISTAKES:** We're all going to make mistakes. This is part of the mindset of someone who really cares deeply about seeing everyone brought into agreement and community around this work—our goals should not be to guilt, shame, or blame but to teach, to add clarity, and to bring people along. We can't do that if we're attacking people. That's why I say I don't like cancel culture. It does not serve us well. But I absolutely believe in accountability and in transparency.

- **DON'T SPEAK FOR OTHERS:** Be sure to use *I* and *me* statements to speak on behalf of yourself. Do not speak on behalf of someone else. I like to clarify that point, because at the crux of inclusion and belonging is allowing, not denying, people their individuality. We often assume we know what they're trying to communicate, and sometimes we're right and sometimes we're wrong. Let them center their voice.

- ⚙ **CLARITY IS KIND:** Remember that resistance is often a result of a lack of clarity. Overcommunicate, especially around topics that we know can create some discomfort and tension points. But do it with a great level of empathy and compassion so that people feel like you are supporting this growth and learning journey. Clarity allows us to help instead of having people feel they may be shunned or shamed or guilted. This also minimizes any trepidation people may have about speaking up.

- ⚙ **WHERE YOU SIT DETERMINES WHAT YOU SEE:** Where you sit within an organization will determine what you see. Power dynamics automatically create a potential situation where there is a huge perception of a lack of empathy, compassion, and thoughtfulness. Some people may believe that you're sitting up in an ivory tower just making decisions and having it all trickle down.

DEI in action says, "Nothing about me without me." If I belong to an underrepresented population and I feel that my interest, my lived experience, is not something that you are aware of and holding in mind, then I'm going to perceive that you are not operating from a

> **DEI in action says, "Nothing about me without me."**

place of leadership by considering how this impacts me and people like me. I'm going to believe you're making decisions without even considering me and without even being thoughtful about what my needs are, what my pain points are.

Leaders must evaluate whether they're being thoughtful enough to walk the hall, to seek inclusive feedback as they're making decisions, and whether they extend open-door policies where they can be accessible. A lot of leaders leverage town hall meetings and send out weekly or biweekly email communication that provides a connection point. Is there a way for people to provide feedback that trickles *back up* to all those decision makers? This is where it's valuable to have a DEI council with a vetted and appointed subset of leaders who are enacted to be the voice and the soul of the broader community. Efforts like that show a level of thoughtfulness, consideration, and commitment to center as many voices as possible from a leadership perspective.

- **AVOID POLITICAL CORRECTNESS:** People will drive toward political correctness, and I think that does us no good. What we need to be doing is teaching people how to build up their cultural intelligence. If someone is sharing some information and a part of that information is harmful, maybe it's because it's rooted in some level of bias or stereotypes or generalizations about a population of people. If another person can treat that as an opportunity to teach through storytelling, I believe that can shift the outcome.

- **IT'S NOT ABOUT VOCABULARY:** We can keep shifting and changing the language almost as though if we make it a little bit softer, we can bring more people along. I tend to think it's just going to create another set of challenges. We can add a whole bunch of other alphabets to DEI, but at the core, the work and the need for the work is pretty much going to stay the same. It's about centering humanity and respect and opportunity for all. We have to get rid of the rhetoric. It can't just be talk. We must be able to align our rhetoric with action.

- **MINDFUL SITUATIONAL AWARENESS:** Let's say you're in a group think tank or general meeting and talking about different engagement opportunities happening within the organization. Perhaps your millennial colleagues are not feeling inclined to share, so you invite their participation to the conversation. "Shaun, I haven't heard from you. Kesha, I haven't heard from you. I would love to get your thoughts on this as well."

  If the meeting is small enough, I would recommend doing a round-robin when you can. That's not always possible, but it gives everyone an opportunity to center their voice; even if they feel reluctant, they can always pass. Give people an opportunity to join the discussion later. Maybe they're still processing. Be intentional about making people feel comfortable, and give them an open opportunity to share.

- **AMPLIFICATION:** We see this often with women and younger professionals. Once they've said something, their words are kind of glossed over, or someone who is more senior, perhaps a white male, will then go back and repeat it or offer some variation of it, and then everybody's like, "That's a great idea."

  That's an opportunity to say, "Well, so-and-so said this a while back." Trace the thread back to the original weaver.

137

Amplification—amplifying what colleagues are saying, particularly colleagues whose voices are often lost and missing from the conversation—fosters a culture of speaking up. They will perceive they have allies who in future situations might again amplify and give them credit. That builds confidence and allows them to believe that "Okay, if it falls flat on many others, maybe there's one person who will see fit to amplify my voice."

● **RESPECT AND CHALLENGE:** In a culture of speaking up, we don't usually consider that it's also about respectfully (and I use that word very intentionally) challenging the status quo. We don't know what we don't know, so sometimes it's necessary to ask thoughtful questions like "Tell me more about that," or "What causes you to feel that way?" or "Do you have an example of what you are expressing?"

These are respectful, noninvasive ways of challenging people's thinking, especially if it's rooted in bias or potential harm. Questioning and challenging the status quo is an act of a bravery. It can be incredibly courageous. Choose courage over comfort.

● **GIVE GRACE, AND ACCEPT GRACE:** People are entering these conversations at different places. Instead of assuming the way the words landed on us was the way the person intended them, we need to extend grace. We're going to make mistakes ourselves as well.

Extending grace looks like assuming positive intent. Let that foster curiosity to ask questions, which is instrumental to dialogue and gets us to clarity. There's hopefully learning occurring on both ends. Extending grace and accepting grace is important because it helps to shut down the notion that "I don't want to speak up because I'm afraid I may say the wrong thing."

- **HOLD THE NUANCES:** Our ability to help bring people along has a lot to do with our tolerance and our willingness to hold the middle. Sometimes it's the power of "both/and." Value the nuance throughout the process, and hold the middle to amplify the common ground.

- **ACCEPTANCE:** Tension points exist in us when we feel there is a right, wrong, good, or bad way instead of "that's right for you." Until it starts infringing upon the human rights of others, I have to respect that that's right for you. This point sometimes gets lost. Acceptance doesn't always mean agreement.

- **SAY THANK YOU:** Thank people for sharing. "Thank you for sharing that perspective." Even as you're giving that constructive, positive feedback, as you're thanking them for sharing, be explicit about what enlightened you or what added value. Again, that piece of thoughtfulness and consideration goes one step deeper than just the surface.

- **COMMIT TO ACTUALIZING IDEAS:** Remember our intention to shift from activity to impact? Let's call that out. More impactful than thanking them in a very specific way is committing to actualizing their ideas. And now you have a legacy.

An organization that I worked for got an award, and it was because twelve months prior I had initiated an idea that continued to grow and develop and add value. Every time that idea was talked about, credit was given back to me. It just built up this greater groundswell of the value that I provided, and I think that's important. Little things like that add up and can make a difference. That simple act of acknowledgment can be really powerful.

Forward Momentum

Organizations need to do training that goes deeper. For example, let's say someone from an underrepresented group speaks up about being gaslit and how it caused them to shut down, to feel dismissed and dissuaded from sharing other important thoughts. We need to educate on that. Maybe there's training on what it looks like to gaslight team members, how that harm shows up, and what we need to do about it.

A lot of leaders in organizations do not look like that colleague and have no clue about gaslighting. They have experienced it neither in the same way nor to the intensity that the underrepresented colleague has. The implications are that when you gaslight, microaggressions are happening, and that can cause marginalized groups to feel silenced and fearful of sharing.

That goes back again to psychological safety. Psychological safety is key to supporting those groups and giving them the space to express their ideas without holding them in situations where they're harboring stress. "I want to say this. I know I should say it because it's going to help show my thought leadership, my value to the organization, but I won't."

This just perpetuates the continual bigger problem. It also leads to a lack of opportunities. A lack of visibility creates a lack of awareness about and exposure to what people have to offer. There's a lot to unpack as we deepen the work:

- Do we allow individuals to come together through these safe spaces and discussion groups where they're processing together what they heard and how they feel about what they heard?

- Are there tools that can be leveraged so people can begin to actualize and apply some of the information they learned?

- What are the takeaways, and how can we ensure it's not just "I came; I was inspired; I was moved; I learned something," and then the following week, "I can't really repeat anything about it"?

- How do we continually approach DEI comprehensively and drive toward impact?

We must be constantly building and activating a strategy that helps people deepen their knowledge and understanding. There's always another level … and another level.

Employee Life Cycle

With all that in mind, organizations must position DEI within the full employee life cycle from beginning to end. It must start during the recruitment planning process of candidates and feature in the types of conversations that occur during the interview period to ensure there's alignment of value.

What are the guiding principles the organization decides are critical for employees? Has the organization really evaluated their current culture and identified the gaps or opportunities to further embed DEI, and have they aligned accordingly? If not, then you can expect to attract people who may come in being indifferent or even seeing DEI as a distraction or as unimportant.

Organizations must consider how they're leveraging DEI brand assets and reinforcing an inclusive mindset at every stage of the employee's growth. That includes the DEI statement, the way the company speaks and embeds culture and environment, and the way they utilize marketing pieces from recruitment through internal communications so everyone from new hires to seasoned company veterans knows the importance of DEI to the organization. This furthers the continuous cycle of progress that feeds back into the organization, its employees, and the public it serves.

Expect Nonclosure

There will not be one book, webinar, or conference that allows you to completely get it. It's my hope that this book is enough to elicit a foundation of curiosity and offers sufficient tools to encourage self-agency around what you can do next. Take what you've heard and learned, and then actualize and put into practice what you can—right now. Remember that transforming culture is a journey, not a destination. Accepting nonclosure provides a continual opportunity for improvement.

Hybrid and Remote Work

One organizational shift that holds great opportunity for improvement occurred during the pandemic. Hybrid and remote work became standard practices during the pandemic and have changed the future of work forever. Hybrid or even fully remote working arrangements can play an important role in organizations' diversity, equity, inclusion, and belonging strategies.

Potential Solutions

Flexible and hybrid work—if done right—can be vital tools in the quest for equity in the workplace.

BREAKING DOWN LOCATION BARRIERS

Without the restriction of location, organizations have the liberty to recruit diverse talent from anywhere around the globe. Similarly, employees can choose where they want to operate based on factors such as location preference, cost of living, and proximity to family and friends.

CLOSING THE GENDER GAP

Remote operations offer better opportunities and greater flexibility for women. Remote work can be especially attractive to single, working mothers, enabling more women to pursue professional careers.

MAKING IT EASY FOR WORKERS WITH DISABILITIES

Millions of people live with disabilities. It is common for people with disabilities to pass on an opportunity for which they're qualified because of challenges related to commuting, accessibility within the workplace, and more. Working remotely allows employees to work in an atmosphere that's more customized to their needs.

ELIMINATING VISUAL BIAS IN THE WORKPLACE

Visual bias leads to assumptions about a person based on their appearance, such as skin color, hairstyle, fashion, tattoos, etc. Such visual bias may make it challenging for some to find work or advance in their careers. Remote work helps eliminate the visual element from work. This becomes even more beneficial if it relates to race, ethnicity, gender, and sexual orientation—in a remote working environment, these visual biases are less apparent.

Plausible Problems

Despite advantages, remote work also has the potential to reveal and exacerbate inequity in our workplaces.

LIMITED ACCESS TO LEADERS

Face time with decision makers is crucial for anyone's career trajectory. While one-on-one and team meetings can certainly have a common frequency whether on Zoom or in the office, employees choosing to work two or three days from home lack the opportunity for ad hoc meetings and conversations. In-office employees can more easily develop rapport, where a vice president passing them in the aisle on the way to the conference room could say, "Why don't you come in and listen—you may pick up some useful context." Meanwhile, the employee working from home on that day simply isn't top of mind to be invited.

FAVORING IN-OFFICE EMPLOYEES

Proximity bias is the tendency for people in positions of authority to show favoritism or give preferential treatment to employees who are closest to them physically. Proximity bias is a mental shortcut that allows managers to make decisions about performance, promotions, and hiring based on familiarity rather than objective criteria.

Common examples of proximity bias include the following:

- Evaluating the work of on-site employees more highly than remote employees regardless of objective performance metrics

- Offering the most interesting projects, assignments, or development opportunities to on-site employees

- Excluding remote employees from important meetings or not encouraging them to speak up on calls

ENCOURAGING LESS DIVERSE OFFICE SPACES

All underrepresented groups experience microaggressions in the workplace. There is nothing micro about microaggressions. Even when these are the result of good intentions, they still have an impact. Think about all the ways people can feel more themselves at home: Employees who identify as nonbinary can more easily display pronouns on their Zoom screen than face the awkward statements face to face. A nursing mother can avoid being asked how long she plans to breastfeed when taking a moment to pump. Differently abled people don't encounter unnecessary offers of assistance.

Now, think about who is most likely to favor working in the office. They are the employees with the fewest barriers to doing so—predominately able-bodied, white, cisgender males.

From Problems to Solutions

Thoughtful action can help teams build new habits, strengthen connections, and encourage the growth of inclusive cultures that will better realize the full potential of all employees.

One of the mistakes we're making about remote work is assuming that it means the same thing for everyone. This isn't just considering where people work, but how. It won't be enough to provide equal access to laptops, mobile phones, and an internet connection. Instead, we must recognize and design new ways of working to empower employees, provide opportunity, and meet them where they are.

Positive Practices

It's imperative to create concrete strategies to sustain and strengthen diversity, equity, inclusion, and belonging in your new remote work environment. Remember that some employees may feel like an untethered strand in hybrid or remote work environments while others will feel more freedom. We must acknowledge the differences and ensure we're weaving connection into our digital spaces in ways that are effective for everyone.

DEMONSTRATE VULNERABILITY AND EMPATHY

Get to know team members on a more personal level by asking open-ended questions on topics they care about. Allocate time each week to do a physical-emotional-intellectual (PEI) check-in.

ASK ABOUT PEOPLE'S NEEDS, ACKNOWLEDGE THEM, AND TAILOR ACTIONS ACCORDINGLY

Establish direct communication with coworkers who may feel like "onlys," see how they are doing, and make a point to draw them into discussions. Be brave and address the "elephant in the room": acknowledge difficult situations, ask questions, and create space for people to share openly how they are feeling and what they need.

CHALLENGE PERSONAL ASSUMPTIONS, ADOPT A LEARNING ORIENTATION, AND SEEK TO UNDERSTAND OTHERS' EXPERIENCES AND PERSONAL STYLES

Ask questions before asserting rather than assuming someone's experience. Acknowledge what you don't know, and express a desire to learn more.

BUILD SPACE FOR DIVERSE PERSPECTIVES, AND ENCOURAGE GREATER PARTICIPATION

Send out an agenda for the meeting ahead of time with clearly defined roles and content topics. Give credit where it's due—when an individual reiterates an idea that someone else put forward earlier in the meeting, point out who shared the idea originally.

MAKE TIME FOR STRUCTURED REMOTE TEAM BUILDING AND NETWORKING

Set up semiregular remote sessions dedicated solely to familiarizing team members with one another. Develop exercises or games that encourage interactions with unfamiliar team members.

BE INTENTIONAL ABOUT MENTORING AND DEVELOPING ALL TEAM MEMBERS

Schedule regular one-on-one check-ins to discuss how individual team members are doing, assess their goals and interests, and explore their professional development intentions. Increase transparency of opportunities by asking the whole team for volunteers.

ENCOURAGE TEAM MEMBERS TO SET INDIVIDUAL INCLUSION COMMITMENTS

Everyone plays a role in creating a more inclusive working environment. Leaders should reinforce this priority, establish accountability, and encourage experimentation with new behaviors.

- -

Critical REFLECTION

Here is a contract called the "Individual Inclusion Commitment." Use it as a guideline to reflect on how you may enter your work life in a different way moving forward:

I will … this week. Please hold me accountable.

 INVEST IN THE WELL-BEING AND FAIR TREATMENT OF OTHERS

- Ensure people get the credit they deserve, and clarify who raised an idea.

- Return the conversation to someone who has been talked over or interrupted.

- Pay attention to who is not speaking, and actively bring them into the dialogue.

- Suspend judgment when someone behaves differently, and seek to understand their actions and motivation.

BECOME AN ALLY TO AND ADVOCATE FOR TARGETS OF MISTREATMENT

- Draw attention to symbolic reminders of male-dominated work culture (for example, "bro talk" or references to women as "girls").

- Draw attention to the use of "other" language within or outside the group.

- Stand up for others if you see instances of noninclusive behavior.

- Lead with curiosity, and seek to understand perspectives different from your own.

- Listen intently, and draw attention to interruptions.

- Invite different opinions to help you learn—after sharing a viewpoint, explicitly ask if there are any additional perspectives you should consider.

- Ask questions to learn more, and share what you understand to make others feel heard.

SUPPORT OTHERS TO ACHIEVE THEIR GOALS

- Volunteer to take on "office housework" (for example, taking notes and organizing events) so it doesn't always fall to the same person.

- Take the time to share advice or knowledge from your experience with others.

- Establish common language to celebrate inclusive behavior, or draw attention to noninclusive behavior in the moment without implying judgment. For example, as a team, select videoconferencing tools or a word or term to call out noninclusive behavior.

- Set up an end-of-week reflection (or include one in existing meetings) to celebrate positive changes and areas for continued growth as a team and to reinforce a more inclusive environment.

It's not about **PROGRAMS OR INITIATIVES.**

Set expectations. **It's never a one-and-done.**

Take time to **DEFINE TERMS.**

Commit to valuing ***diversity of thought.***

The *greatest gift* you can give another person is to simply include them.

Foster a culture of SPEAKING UP.

 Create PSYCHOLOGICAL *safety.*

Dialogue is an asset; **use it responsibly.**

 SPEAK UP.
The only **WRONG THING** you can do is **STAY SILENT** when it matters the most.

TAKE UP *space.*

 Overcommunicate WITH empathy and compassion.

Healthy ego can be a **superpower** for **marginalized populations.**

Remember

- Exercise community agreements.
- Create safe space.
- Be okay with mistakes.
- Don't speak for others.
- Clarity is kind.
- Where you sit determines what you see.
- Avoid political correctness.
- It's not about vocabulary.
- Practice mindful situational awareness.
- Amplify.
- Respect and challenge.
- Give grace; accept grace.
- Say thank you.
- Commit to actualizing ideas.

CHAPTER 8:

Inclusion Is Leadership

The time is always right to do what is right.

—MARTIN LUTHER KING JR.

Inclusive leaders have the ability to create significant change within their organizations. The following is just one example of feedback I've received from senior leadership:

"Dr. Nika White, I wish to say thank you for the positive impact you have had on myself and my work family. When I saw the results of your deep-dive assessment report, it made me feel heard. It made so many of the staff feel heard for the first time. Your report has continued to encourage staff to find their voice and to advocate for their experiences and needs. My best wishes to you and your family."

This is a great example of leadership leaning in, being willing to gather the data, hearing the voices, and then starting to create a culture where people feel they can be heard and seen. They can speak up and name the hard things. It improves every *aspect of the health of an organization.*

This leader went on to say, "There's now a form of unity and support among the staff. I'm truly inspired by your work journey and message. It brings me hope, and it has led me to pursue a PhD in cultural identity development."

Our culture praises leaders who take risks and win big. The most prominent CEOs and media icons have reached where they are today by taking big risks on their values and being intentional with their actions. Society rewards those rare true leaders who are willing to put themselves on the line to make life better for others.

Society rewards those rare true leaders who are willing to put themselves on the line to make life better for others.

Things become a little more complex when we touch on social issues, and we don't consider certain leaders to be experts. We might worry how taking a stance will impact an organization's brand or bottom line. Yet, by taking these risks, leaders of social change often change the game for their industries and for the public at large.

When leaders who are not necessarily known as social activists leverage their platform to exert influence, they have a huge impact on the way society responds to an issue. For example, musician John Legend and activist Rachel Cargle have both amplified the work during these last years by becoming prominent leaders of social change.

A Shift in Language

Many leaders were called to action for the first time after George Floyd's murder. It was so visual and so hard that some organizational leaders who had not initially seen the need to be vocal completely changed their perspective. They decided that as large brands, they had influence and power. They did not want to sit in silence.

We started seeing a shift in language. Some organizations changed their titling or labeling of corporate social responsibility to corporate social justice. That was a sign that organizations realized they do, in fact, have influence to leverage and that with this comes responsibility. They wanted to take the risk of sending a strong message that they value inclusion and equity and care about humanity and social complex issues.

They were doing that in a multitude of ways. People were placing ads in prominent newspapers. They were going to social media. CEOs were writing elaborate letters to express their position and sending it out to the team and having town hall meetings.

Many people ask me which leader stepped up in the aftermath of George Floyd's murder and got it right. Not one organizational leader stands out who I feel hit it on all cylinders. There was so much criticism around that time because people were just reacting, and it was a mess. Every DEI practitioner was inundated during that time with requests for support.

What it did, however, was create an opportunity for people to get into the dialogue, to start having these conversations. That's important, because while they may have fumbled, the hope is that through this fumbling, learning took place and opportunities emerged to better crystallize what this means to leadership and to the organization's commitment to DEI.

The benefit is the story of what was uncovered after the fumbles and what is taking place now. We've seen a deepened commitment from many organizations. While it may not still perfectly align with all the best practices, it's progress. We're after progress and not perfection.

Slow Adoption

Some are still not willing to take the risk of getting involved with what feels like complex social issues. C-suite leaders do understand there are significant risks with DEI. I remember hearing clients say, "Well, our board does not see the relevance of that." They remained stuck.

Sometimes it takes risks when you're managing up, even if you're managing up from the C-suite to your board. It may take effort to help them see the importance and significance of this work of diversity, equity, and inclusion in a meaningful way.

So, yes. There is a risk that many leaders sense they'll have to take, and I don't want that to be missed. The responses from inside the organization and outside the organization will vary.

Some may criticize, "Shame on them for just now arriving after a man is murdered and is visible for everyone." Others may say, "Okay, so it stirred up something. What are we going to do with it now? The table has been set in a different way."

No matter the response, true leaders take risks. Be on the correct side of humanity. Choose courage over comfort.

Inclusion Is Leadership

When we think of leadership traits, we often think of vision, strength, insight, and strong decision-making capacities. I believe we need to add *inclusion* to that list as an essential leadership attribute. Being inclusion minded should not only be encouraged but should also be expected. It's a key ingredient of sustainable leadership in our lives individually and collectively.

Organizations must stop treating the work of DEI as the sole responsibility of the diversity officer and make it a mandate for every person within the organization. Regardless of your title, if you consider yourself a leader or simply a person of influence, you must become inclusion minded and begin to exercise intentionality in doing your individual part to create inclusive environments. This is necessary if we want to become part of the change we want to see.

A leader has a unique and unparalleled opportunity to be the slipknot. When weaving together an inclusive culture, the slipknot is the first and original knot that the entire structure is built upon. Its strength and integrity is what allows all strands to twist and entwine and work together in solidarity. If the slipknot is weak, threads pull apart, they fray, they break down.

Regardless of whether we are in a title or position of leader, we all manage ourselves as we manage our workload, which could include managing different projects, different processes. As the owner and the manager of those processes and projects, are we being intentional to seek thought partnership from others? Are we seeking input from those who have different experiences and perspectives?

If we are, that is inclusive leadership behavior and inclusive influence. We are not just saying, "This is the way I think about this." We are ensuring the final product, the final process, the final project considers different communities and different people who will be impacted.

From an inclusive leadership perspective, I ask, "Are you best equipped and poised to be able to speak on behalf of certain populations of people?" I believe that within the broad conversation of diversity, equity, and inclusion, we do need to be factual. We must make sure we are seeing the humanity and letting that guide us.

From a strategic perspective, we also need to lead with intellect, which means we need to be asking questions. We need to be researching, bringing facts and data to the conversations to help inform a path-forward plan—"How do we do this, and how do we do this effectively so that it can be sustained?"

There's no such thing as getting it right, right away. A lot of times, people will look for a blueprint. "If I do this, this, and this and check those off, then I have arrived." There's no such thing.

The entryway into this work requires us to allow people to be at a place where they can try things, refine, try again. Maybe it's the season, it's the timing. Maybe it's the people that you've assembled. It's helping people understand that while the work is complicated, we combat that by allowing ourselves some level of fluidity to make mistakes. Otherwise, we will remain stuck in the "I can't take even the first step without all the *I*'s being dotted, all the *T*'s being crossed" mindset. That is not realistic.

Take the risks. Use whatever intel you've gathered, and just take the first step. A meaningful DEI journey will always manifest.

Feedback for Leadership

The people in the organization who most need to hear feedback are the ones who are in upper-level leadership positions. They're the ones who can change systems and produce better outcomes. They're the ones who can help foster and deepen accountability if someone's not aligning with the culture, including if *they* are that person.

Sometimes leaders consciously or unconsciously use psychological safety to dodge accountability, for themselves and for others. A problem occurs when people hide behind issues that come up in the workplace. People in positions of leadership may feel ashamed about being accountable for concerns that come up. Accountability and shame are not the same things. We'll address that shortly. Overall, the idea of holding folks accountable when ideas, concerns, and thoughts come up isn't something to run from. It's something to dive deeper into.

Inclusive culture is not only about allowing people to feel safe, to share their thoughts and their opinions. If leaders are in the room, can they disagree with a policy or have a dissenting point of view? Can they respectfully present that opinion to leadership and know there will not be repercussions? This goes back to the conformity piece.

How do leaders respond when met with what's perceived as criticism or constructive candor? Even if it means they are faced with making fundamental changes that impact the company as a whole? Feedback or criticism from any corner of the corporation should be considered a safe and welcome practice.

Inclusion in Accountability

As an inclusive leader, holding yourself and others accountable is necessary to further the work of DEI. Holding someone accountable doesn't require shaming or berating them in front of their colleagues to prove a point. There are real and tangible ways you can have an honest and effective conversation with your employees without anyone retreating into shame, anger, and defensiveness.

UNDERSTAND THAT PEOPLE MAY NOT KNOW THEY'VE CAUSED HARM TO OTHERS

The truth is, many people say and do harmful things, and they may not know they've done something wrong.

It's important to understand that harm is inevitable because people are often operating unconsciously. In other words, folks are on autopilot when it comes to their speech and behavior, and what comes out of their mouths may not seem harmful to them. But as it turns out, what they did or said was very harmful, and someone else has to check them on it.

The key to beginning the process of holding someone accountable is to move with empathy. Both people should understand that making mistakes is a part of being human. And both parties should also move mindfully through these conversations.

FOCUS ON THE BEHAVIOR OR ACTION, *NOT* THE PERSON

This is important because a lot of people react to being called in as a defect in their character or personality. But it's not. They're not the problem. The problem was their words or actions, which can be changed. When you're calling someone in, focus on what was said or done and on how those actions created the issue. Create a separation between the person's actions and their inherent value as a human.

The reality is, some people aren't culturally competent and may not have the language to respectfully move in certain spaces. It's a fact that hurt people hurt people. Underneath oppressive remarks, slurs, and comments is, oftentimes, someone acting from a place of hurt. Having empathy for a person who's hurting doesn't make what they said or did right, but it does show us a path forward to responding, and it opens us up to being more thoughtful about our approach to behavioral change.

When holding someone accountable, it's also important to understand the difference between responding and reacting. Reacting means having no thought of the long-term consequences of an action. Responding means being more mindful about effective strategies to increase the likelihood of behavior change.

In the case of calling someone in and holding them accountable, we want to respond, not react. We want to make it clear that what was said or done was harmful, and this is why. Reacting with anger, shame, or resentment will likely increase the temperature in the room and encourage defensiveness in the receiving party. Which is helpful for no one and won't improve the situation.

It's not easy to call someone in with respect and kindness, but it's necessary in this work. Many people feel ashamed at the moment and can react poorly to being called out. But it's important for you to practice empathy and self-control in moments like this, because the ultimate goal is to encourage a change in behavior.

HELPFUL PHRASES TO USE WHEN HOLDING SOMEONE ACCOUNTABLE

So, if you're ready to have the hard conversation with someone in a respectful and effective way, here are a few phrases you can use to open up the conversation:

- "Tell me more about the way you're thinking."

- "Help me to understand your perspective."

- "What caused you to feel that way?"

- "What do you mean by that?"

- "That's not a part of our culture."

- "That's not okay with me, and I respect you enough to let you know."

- "Have you considered the harm your words and behaviors can cause to others?"

- "I'm telling you this because I believe that on the issue of bias, we can all learn. It takes a brave spirit for someone to bring forth that constructive feedback."

IF YOU (AS LEADERSHIP) ARE BEING CALLED IN OR HELD ACCOUNTABLE, KNOW YOU'RE NOT THE VICTIM

Once someone has been called in and both parties are aware of the problem, the mindset should be this: "What will my response be now that I'm aware?"

Getting called in can make some people defensive, fearful, or feel that others are gaslighting them. In essence, we, as people being called in, become the victims. But we have to realize that we're not the victims. The person who is holding us accountable is sharing this issue with us because a change is necessary in order to reach equity, inclusion, and compassion. There's no shame in admitting we've brought harm to someone else and that it wasn't right. But it's important to adapt to the feedback we're receiving and integrate it.

Having empathy for yourself and understanding that biases occur within all of us is another key step. We can't avoid it. Acknowledging that harm has been done is crucial. When an issue is brought to our attention, we need to think about how that harm has created negative consequences for the other person, the person who's really the victim.

So we should ask ourselves this: "What do the people I harmed need at this moment?"

Don't fall into the trap of feeling rushed to be forgiven by the person who called you out. Sometimes your actions or words were so harmful that people aren't ready to forgive yet. So, give people their space, and respect the time it takes to circle back and begin the process of forgiveness.

If you're the one being held accountable, it's important you take responsibility and make sure no future harm is created:

- Apologize.

- Feel atonement.

- Acknowledge the harm.

- Commit to stopping the cycle.

- Meet with company leadership to ensure accountability.

- Create a plan to change what needs amending as leadership or as an organization.

- Communicate those changes across all levels of the organization.

Most importantly, don't do this work alone. Seek reassurance and support from people who are there for you. Connect with your community, and talk out what happened. Ask if they've been through the same thing or how they've handled it. Seek to understand, reflect, and course correct. But don't shame yourself for what you didn't know. Now you do know, so you can make better choices in the future, and that's what really matters.

Optimize, Not Weaponize

Remember last chapter when we spoke of holding the middle, giving and getting grace, and resting in acceptance? These practices apply to all involved in the DEI conversation.

Instead of demonizing people for potential and initial performative actions—no matter their level of leadership—how do we make sure we provide support and guidance so the change they make is real? So the words they put out have weight to stand on?

I believe it begins with recognizing and standing firmly that "the main goal is the main goal."

The main goal is to work toward creating equity in society, business, and life. To bring as many people along as possible. To leave no one behind.

We have to go back to our *why* when confronted with what could be perceived on the surface as performative. We must see that as an opportunity to help educate and bring awareness to the potential harm. The main goal is not to weaponize people or cause them to back away; it is to facilitate them to do the hard work at its core. Where it's not just about activity but about impact.

Personally, I have been encouraged by the shift in how people are asking about DEI services more and more. It used to be quick requests of "I need a training" or "I need an assessment" or even "I need a way for my Black colleagues to stop complaining about discrimination."

Now, it's more action oriented. People are coming to the table with a longer-term outlook after experiencing a paradigm shift around this work. Instead of those quick requests, people are now saying, "Hey, Dr. Nika. We need a plan that can expand over multiple years and that goes over all elements of our organization so we can deliver on DEI in everything we do."

To me, that sounds much better and like we're making progress. Let's not hinder that progress. We might have to take steps backward if we aren't giving people a safe way to enter the conversation.

How to Offer Support for Those Who Are Just Arriving

The truth is that now is the time. Leaders are more open than ever to take guidance from their chief DEI officers, heads of diversity, HR leaders, and/or DEI consultants. Let's leverage that to the best of our ability. Let's strike while the iron is hot.

As practitioners, as leaders, as allies within our spheres of influence, we must be willing to go on this transformative journey with everyone who shows up. If we're trying to manage up with our internal stakeholders and hoping for them to immediately "get it," it's going to be a more difficult journey.

Everyone has their own style and convictions with the work that we do. For some people, it is to come across intense and combative in the attempt to take down the strong and inherent structures of racism. Others go about it more subtly. A few sit in the middle. Everyone has their own space within this work, and I respect that.

I've always felt that it was important to create a balance between saying what needs to be said without diluting the work while also extending an amount of grace to people who are late to the conversation or not quite as knowledgeable.

We are here to consult and support the shift. As people unlearn the historical, unconscious, and systematized systems of inequity, we must help them think about some of those tough subjects they haven't been able to broach or understand.

That said, it doesn't mean that everyone is going to say, "Yes! We're going to do this work and do everything you said right away!" While DEI is critically important (and what I'm most passionate about), organizational leaders have to make many critical decisions on a daily basis. They are making decisions around global events, the economy, hiring and firing, running the business, etc.—so don't neglect that.

We also need to be willing to manage up and say to C-suite leaders, "The voice of DEI doesn't necessarily have to be the DEI person. It has to be *you*, the CEO. You need to own carrying that banner, and all those who are direct reports will follow the lead."

I always say, "We don't have to own the intent, but we have to own the impact." Leaders of all types are getting a taste of that. What does it mean to own the impact? That can be pretty heavy for people. Many think, *I'm not the one who invented racism.* True. You didn't invent it, but you are benefiting from it. If you are a white person in society today, you are benefiting from the history and systems of racism. So, even if you didn't participate in or invent the systems, you do benefit from them. Own the impact.

DEI *Improves Marketability*

DEI plans look good on paper, but stakeholders, future employees, and other parties are looking for proof of your company's dedication to the work.

As mentioned earlier, always leading with the business case can be harmful. Humanity shouldn't have to be justified with a business case, and yet it is an effective way to foster engagement in DEI efforts. When you align company policies and practices with both the moral imperative and the business imperative, you set the organization up for long-term success.

Your leadership team can also be seen as champions of diversity, equity, and inclusion and your company as a wonderful place to work and to partner with. It sends a powerful message to prospects when they see your company taking DEI seriously.

It also sets a positive tone that can include the marketability of your company in the long run.

You have greater ability to attract the best talent, and when you have the best talent, that obviously puts you in a position where you can be incredibly competitive because your outputs, your products, your services are going to benefit from that.

Generally speaking, we are seeing that a lot of people have grown accustomed to being part of spaces and environments that value DEI, especially younger generations. They are asking questions in their job search and looking for career growth within companies that have proven practices and policies of equal opportunities.

The business case for DEI speaks for itself. Here are just a few examples:

- Organizations with ethnic and cultural diversity are 36 percent more likely to be profitable than their peers.[17]

- Organizations with gender diversity are 25 percent more likely to be profitable than their peers.

- Diverse employees have up to a 20 percent higher rate of innovation.

- Diverse employees have 19 percent higher innovation revenues.

---

17   Sundiatu Dixon-Fyle, Kevin Dolan, Vivian Hunt, and Sara Prince, "Diversity Wins: How Inclusion Matters," McKinsey.com, May 19, 2020, accessed June 4, 2022, https://www.mckinsey.com/featured-insights/diversity-and-inclusion/diversity-wins-how-inclusion-matters.

Numbers like these allow company leadership and stakeholders to see how diversity impacts the bottom line. Being armed with data is strategic and shows what sustainability looks like on paper.

Corporations are in the business of making money. We can have this great kumbaya moment where everyone feels good. Yet, how do we sustain that "feel good" moment? How do we motivate employees to keep showing up at their best at work? We do that by proving we're willing to make the investments in human capital as well as financial capital.

What is equally true is that while DEI has had a groundswell of interest and newcomers entering the space over these last years, similar to other disciplines it has not been treated as priority. When a company has to downsize or cut the budget, DEI is one of those areas where leaders often say, "Okay, we can get rid of this."

A lot of this has to do with the fact that as practitioners, as advocates, we have not fully leveraged all our strategic, critical-thinking skills to facilitate change in this body of work. Stats on profitability and innovation are huge motivators, and that is important. What's also important is to remember the humanity aspect that's at the core of this work.

DEI work must reflect both sides—intellectual and emotional. As DEI practitioners or champions or allies, let's lead with balance. Let's bring the intellectual insight and intel to better secure and protect the turf of DEI work. Let's also never forget to bring heart to the mission and remember our *why*: to leave no one behind.

Critical REFLECTION

Take a moment to think about a time when you have inadvertently harmed someone or have been called out for something you were unaware caused harm.

Pause and reflect on the following questions:

- What harm was caused?

- What does that mean?

- What was the impact?

- What are the needs of the person who was harmed?

As a leader, what did you do or not do that brought justice or reconciliation to the situation? Was there more to be done? If so, what would you (or will you do) differently within the organization as a result of this constructive feedback?

True leaders **take risks.**

DEI *is* **a risk for** *leadership.*

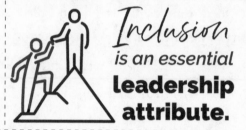

Inclusion is an essential **leadership attribute.**

DEI IS NOT JUST THE MANDATE OF THE

diversity officer.

DEI *is the work of* **EVERYONE** *in* **the organization.**

CHOOSE COURAGE OVER COMFORT.

Remember

- There's no such thing as getting it right, right out of the gate.
- Leaders must listen to constructive feedback.
- Optimize, don't weaponize, people for where they are in the DEI journey.
- Say what needs to be said, and extend grace.
- DEI improves the marketability of your company and leadership.
- Use the business case, and don't forget the humanity.
- Leave no one behind.

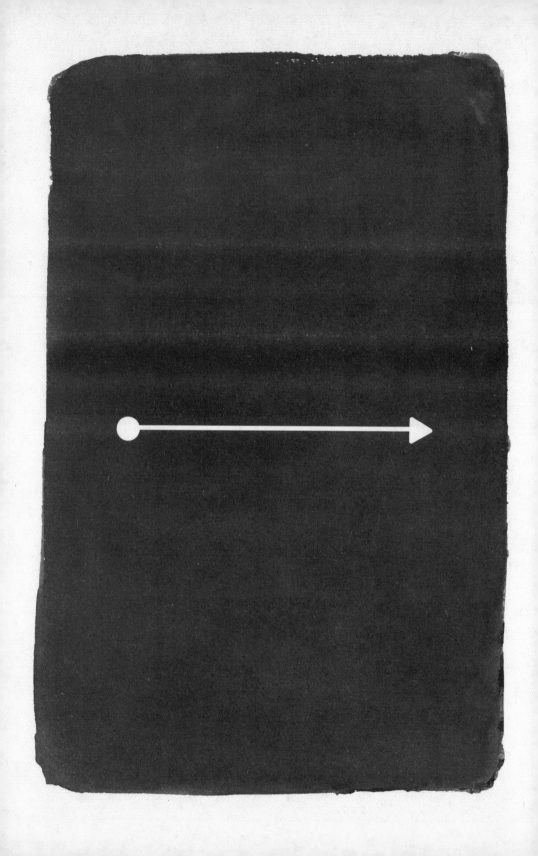

Conclusion

We've unraveled the yarn, teased out the knots, and arrived at the simplest understanding of the DEI work we're engaged in. At this moment.

As you've discovered in our time together, DEI is a transformative journey that never ends. We have gone through the tangled layers of systems of oppression, discovered hidden strands that are frayed and fragile, and found cords of injustice that require urgent and intentional repair.

We've unraveled a lot of misconceptions, traveled lengths of twisted territories, and gotten a little closer to the essence of what DEI means and what it can do for you, for others, and for corporations seeking to make a difference.

As this book comes to a close, I'd like to leave you with some final thoughts and words of encouragement to reflect on, come back to, and remember at every stage of this dynamic and worthy process:

- **The path to transformation begins with a single step.** Remember how complex DEI seemed when you first picked up this book? And now, you've learned practical tools and simple actions you can take right now to begin the work in earnest or to continue deepening your commitment.

The path to transformation begins with a single step—and you've already taken it by journeying this far with me. You are armed with the mindset, the know-how, and the determination to center all voices and to do your part to bring equity into being for all. I know it's a lot, but this resource is always here for you to return to again and again.

⬢ **It's not about perfection; it's about progress.** I know I have said this repeatedly. On purpose. We are all going to make mistakes. There is no one way to "do" DEI. I've given you the best rules of the road I know, and they've proven effective for thousands of leaders and organizations I've consulted with. You can do this. It begins with one step. And then the next, and then the next.

⬢ **Remember the why.** Keep reminding yourself daily of the *why* behind the work of inclusion. We must renew our commitment to the work so that we can continue to fight the good fight. DEI is the responsibility of all of us. The mission is to leave no one behind.

⬢ **Leverage small wins to build momentum.** Recognize that a single victory is not enough to sustain the work of diversity, equity, and inclusion. It must be an ongoing learning process, with practical shifts you can continue to make every day, every week, every month of your life.

Hopefully this book has helped you begin to create a series of actions that can help build your confidence, your speed, and your power.

- **It's a journey and not a destination.** Again, this work is really hard, and it can be exhausting. That's especially true for the individuals who have committed a lot of their influence, their time, and their talents to being a champion of this work. When you remind yourself there's no destination to get to, it allows spaciousness to just do the work and enjoy what is possible along the way.

- **Celebrate the small wins!** Know that you are planting seeds along the way that others are going to nurture and water. They are going to materialize; this work does not happen overnight.

- **Look for the milestones.** The best way to stay the course and not feel defeated, exhausted, or burned out by the work is to identify the milestones along the way that illustrate we are moving in the right direction.

This will help us keep going. It will keep our spirits up and our momentum rolling and give us traction for some loftier goals around the future. What I find is that if we were to really sit and ponder the daunting task of dismantling all these systems that lead to bias, discrimination, marginalization, disenfranchisement ... if all of us really were to sit there long enough, we would feel defeated before we even took the first step.

The reality is, we have to find ways to center ourselves around "What can we do?" and then feel some sense of accomplishment with the milestones we're making along the way. Don't see this as some big ball of complexity. Even just through the steps of this book and applying some of this information, we have already started to unravel that big ball of yarn. So that's a victory in and of itself. If there's a point of loosening knots of tension in your life, in your community, in your workplace—threads that were tangled that have now started to give way—that's unraveling toward liberation and transformation.

Remember, we are developing and contributing to, step by step, other bigger initiatives and work that will foster a deepened sense of commitment to diversity, equity, and inclusion.

🌐 **Transformation occurs over time.** Just think about how much you've absorbed throughout these pages. Now that you've made it, I'm hoping you're thinking to yourself, *Okay, this is the goal: celebrate the milestone, and revel in what's ahead!*

It's my wish that you'll be so refreshed and fueled by this process, you will take a moment and ask, "So, what's next?" because there's always a "next."

This work will never end. If we all are taking responsibility and the onus of this work, we should all feel similarly about it. I often say my greatest wish is to work myself out of a job. What I mean by that is, I want society, people, to all feel a sense of accountability and ownership toward this work, to where we don't have to have special disciplines and people who are helping to force the conversation and the mindset. It is something that should be a normal part of our spaces and how we show up in the world for ourselves and for others.

Celebrate and Continue

You made it! Together, we have unraveled the complexities within each chapter and simplified DEI in a digestible, applicable way. We have gotten closer to the work and closer to the real meaning behind all we do.

We've traveled quite a distance together on this transformative journey, but the work of untangling injustice is just beginning in some ways. I encourage you to celebrate the small wins you've already accomplished and to continue to critically reflect on all you've learned. Rest when needed, but allow this to fuel further action and inspire a greater sense of urgency around this work. Know you are courageously contributing to change with even the smallest of efforts to unravel and undo ties of unrelenting systems of oppression.

Together—with you as an ally, a leader, and an advocate of shared humanity—we will weave the fabric of a stronger, more beautiful, more equitable future for all, leaving no one behind.

APPENDIX:

Chapter Summaries

Since the goal of this book is to un-complicate DEI, I want to leave you with the most important threads of this DEI journey.

Active Opposition

Active opposers are typically deeply rooted in their choice to be a strong opponent of DEI. These are the people whose minds cannot be changed and who are committed to disrupting the work of DEI. The potential for engagement is slim and often leads to the determination that the energy of trying is in vain. My advice is to let them be—there are far too many other people who can be persuaded. Putting our energy into changing the minds of active opposers can cause burnout. The best way to interact with these individuals is to not engage in heated conversation and to show them love in the best way you can, not hate. In the wise words of Dr. Martin Luther King Jr., "I have decided to stick with love. Hate is too great a burden to bear." Light drives out darkness.

Passive Unaware

These are the people who are unaware and cannot engage in the work of DEI, simply because they are uninformed. Passively unaware individuals can be identified by their lack of engagement in the conversation and their inability to recognize the severity of the problems that loom of equity and equality.

If you notice a group discussing the lack of Brown and Black people on a panel, and this person doesn't engage, bring them into the conversation. After getting them to the discussion, if they share, they don't have much to add to the subject or don't have the point of view to weigh in; we can infer that they are passively unaware. This is an opportunity to connect and expose the individual to broader perspective. Reach out to have a one-on-one conversation. Ask questions, share your personal investment in DEI, and listen. Make sure to listen to learn.

Passive Awareness

Passively aware individuals are the ones who can appreciate that attention is being given to the work of DEI but see it as someone else's responsibility—the bystander effect. To illustrate passive awareness, we can use the same situation from passive unawareness.

If you notice a group discussing the lack of Brown and Black people on a panel and this person doesn't engage, bring them into the conversation. After getting them to the discussion, if they express that they realize DEI is essential but trust other people to get the job done, you can recognize passive awareness.

They see this as the work of someone else instead of taking ownership to help solve inequity. Often this disengagement comes from feeling that DEI is about marginalized communities. If someone doesn't identify with a marginalized community, they may be dismissive about their personal accountability.

Because this person is aware of the need to value DEI, they can be persuaded to deepen their engagement and begin to see themselves as part of the solution. Meet them where they are. Invite them for coffee or tea, and have a chat. Ask them questions to suggest entry points of engagement in DEI that feel comfortable to them as they start an intentional journey of modeling inclusive leadership. This is an opportunity to show them their voice matters. They can serve as an ally and be an advocate for change for those in their circle of influence.

Active Awareness

Our actively aware mental modelers are the ones who know this work is necessary and are actively working to advance it. These can be our DEI practitioners, human rights activists, and social justice workers, but they are also regular people who work daily to advocate for others. These individuals work to bring others to the forefront and to make space at the table to center voices that are rarely heard from.

Active awareness can be practiced by speaking up for silenced voices, self-educating through books, documentaries, discussions, etc., and pushing for equity and inclusion in personal and professional spaces. Because the actively aware are so involved, they are the key champions to bringing the passively unaware and passively aware to the party.

Overactive Awareness

At times, active awareness can go a little too far and even sometimes hinder the efforts to advance one's engagement in DEI work. Those who have hyper-awareness are often early adopters of the work, or they have been victimized in such a way that they are headstrong about the work and wish to see results by any means necessary. An example of overactive awareness is cancel culture. If a person/organization shares something offensive, exclusionary, or politically incorrect, this mental model will cancel the person/organization; instead of extending grace and allowing for correction, growth, and progress, these people automatically ostracize.

We are all human. We are going to make mistakes. By going to extremes when a person or organization makes a mistake, we push people further away from this space. While we need to hold people accountable to change and learn from their mistakes, we must extend grace and avoid being overactive or aggressive because aggression will only be met with aggression. When this occurs, we lose all opportunity to influence and increase the likelihood of behavior change. Sure, you want people to do the work of DEI, but do you want them to do it despite or because of?

Humans are 99% identical.

Inclusion recognizes that

All People are entitled to humanity and to dignity. Every voice matters. Every person contributes value.

DEI is **everyone's** Responsibility.

Race + Gender are cultural concepts, **not** biological ones.

There is no finish line.

DEI is a **dynamic, transformational** journey.

DEI *is* **NECESSARY for** *Survival*

DEI IS A LOT MORE THAN *Race + Gender,*

it includes degrees of:

- **Physical Abilities**
- **Sexual Preference**
- **Economics**
- **Trauma**
- **Age**
- **And more...**

There is **no one path** to DEI.

DEI work doesn't imply that white people have not had any **burdens or hardships.**

Remember

- Awareness and reflection
- Be intentional
- Recognize passivity is a barrier to change
- Be open
- Follow the call-to-action
- Understand everyone has bias
- Choose courage over comfort
- Actively seek more information
- Look for the evidence

We are *neurologically hardwired* **for stories.**

EVERYONE has a **DEI STORY.**

We make a lot of *assumptions* about other people.

Their stories help shift our *perspectives.*

We **must make an effort** *to* **get proximate** *to* people's **pain points.**

 PSYCHOLOGICAL SAFETY is needed to *show up, share, and listen* to one another's stories.

 STORIES *connect* **US TO ONE ANOTHER.**

Stories allow us to **WITNESS THE PAIN POINTS** of people with **DIFFERENT LIVED EXPERIENCES** than us.

 Use **NONINVASIVE COMMENTS** to address **POTENTIALLY BIASED REMARKS** or perspectives.

Remember

- Whoever tells the story owns the narrative.
- Examine who is controlling the narrative.
- Collective storytelling unravels the knots.
- Our voices shape the story and identities we want to belong to.
- What do you want people to know about you? About your lived experiences?
- Own your narrative.

Obligation focuses on being a good steward in a surface-level way.

An **OPPORTUNITY MINDSET** *inspires intentionality and commitment to* **MAKE US BETTER HUMANS.**

See *difference* as a *strength.*

EVERYONE IS AT A DIFFERENT POINT IN THE DEI CONVERSATION.

 *Cancel culture* isn't effective in **BRINGING PEOPLE ALONG.**

 **JOB SEEKERS HAVE THE** *upper hand* **AND DEMAND DEI COMMITMENT.**

Remember

- It's not the Great Resignation—it's the Great Reevaluation.
- Companies are going to be forced to commit to DEI if they want to stay viable.
- Don't be afraid of the data.
- Develop multiple modalities, including one-on-one experiences, conversations, sharing of facts.
- Aim for impact over singular activity. Activity has a start and an end date. A mindset shift is growing and ongoing.

We all have bias.

IT DOESN'T MAKE US BAD PEOPLE,
but it **does not exonerate us** from the
consequences of our actions.

Examine
**YOUR
PERSONAL
BIASES**
so you're
**EMPOWERED
TO RESPOND**
instead of
**REACTING TO
DIFFERENCES.**

Bias *is*
involuntary and
instantaneous.

**Any number
of things can
trigger our
reactivity.**

Exclusion
results from bias and
acting on misinformation.

Remember

- Mindfulness is the first step.
- Be diligent, know your triggers, and avoid getting sidetracked by challenges.
- Cultivate mindfulness practices such as awareness and taming the critic.
- Pause before interactions and ask yourself how you want to show up.
- Cultivate cultural intelligence.
- Focus on restorative instead of punitive justice.
- Speed is the bias enabler.
- Organizations have bias.
- Understand systemic bias and its consequences on other populations.

To be an ally, you must first *understand* systems of oppression.

PERFORMATIVE ALLYSHIP usually includes an **easy-to-do one-off** activity.

THINK ABOUT ALL THE "ISMS":

- *Sexism*
- *Racism*
- *Heterosexism*
- *Ableism*
- *Classism*
- *Ageism*

True allyship

is a process of **building relationships** based upon **trust, consistency, and accountability** with the **marginalized identities we seek to support and empower.**

Get proximate to the problem.

BEING A *good ally* **TAKES INTENTION AND USEFUL ACTION.**

Solidarity

means you are being active in **HELPING TO FACILITATE A CHANGE.**

Remember

- Progress is not perfection.
- Seek out marginalized voices and perspectives to gain better cultural competence.
- Don't just talk the work. Do the work.
- Confront racism/bigotry, and do it with a high level of intolerance.
- As a community or business, have a high compass for social consciousness.
- Give up time and money to support organizations and nonprofits that do this work.
- Be vocal, and call out inequities and poor behavior.
- Do the internal allyship work, not just the external.

Privilege *is the absence of barriers and the presence of* **UNEARNED ADVANTAGES.**

Power **often goes hand in hand with** *privilege.*

Sources of **POWER AND PRIVILEGE** include being part of **dominant ethnic or racial groups, being male, being cisgender.**

Equity refers to **fair access, opportunity, advancement, and just practices and policies** that **ensure every person can thrive.**

KNOW YOUR SOURCES OF POWER AND PRIVILEGE.

Acknowledging **POWER AND PRIVILEGE** allows you to **EMPOWER OTHERS.**

If you are a member of **dominant** *culture, you have* *white privilege.*

Failure to **acknowledge** *privilege* **leads to** *bias and* **oppressive behaviors.**

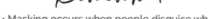

Remember

- Masking occurs when people disguise who they are.
- We must create spaces where people feel a sense of acceptance as whole individuals.
- Create a culture that finds healthy conflict to be normal.
- Once you create more diversity, you must manage diversity.
- Give people full liberty to disagree both with each other and with leadership.
- Shout it out from the rooftops—be vocal everywhere.
- Create a feeling of belongingness.
- Be mindful in the workplace.
- Use intellect over emotion.

It's not about **PROGRAMS OR INITIATIVES.**

Set expectations. **It's never a one-and-done.**

Take time to **DEFINE TERMS.**

Commit to valuing ***diversity of thought.***

The *greatest gift* you can give another person is to simply include them.

Foster a culture of SPEAKING UP.

 Create PSYCHOLOGICAL *safety.*

Dialogue is an asset; **use it responsibly.**

 SPEAK UP. The only **WRONG THING** you can do is **STAY SILENT** when it matters the most.

TAKE UP *space.*

 Overcommunicate WITH empathy and compassion.

Healthy ego can be a ***superpower*** for **marginalized populations.**

 *Remember*

- Exercise community agreements.
- Create safe space.
- Be okay with mistakes.
- Don't speak for others.
- Clarity is kind.
- Where you sit determines what you see.
- Avoid political correctness.
- It's not about vocabulary.
- Practice mindful situational awareness.
- Amplify.
- Respect and challenge.
- Give grace; accept grace.
- Say thank you.
- Commit to actualizing ideas.

True leaders **take risks.**

DEI *is* **a risk for** *leadership.*

Inclusion is an essential **leadership attribute.**

DEI IS NOT JUST THE MANDATE OF THE

diversity officer.

DEI *is the work* *of* **EVERYONE** *in* *the organization.*

CHOOSE COURAGE OVER COMFORT.

Remember

- There's no such thing as getting it right, right out of the gate.
- Leaders must listen to constructive feedback.
- Optimize, don't weaponize, people for where they are in the DEI journey.
- Say what needs to be said, and extend grace.
- DEI improves the marketability of your company and leadership.
- Use the business case, and don't forget the humanity.
- Leave no one behind.

NIKA WHITE CONSULTING

Nika White Consulting is a full-service diversity, equity, and inclusion boutique consulting firm with global reach and recognized authority on strategic diversity, intentional inclusion, and lens of equity. Here are some of the more common services we provide to assist clients across varied industries and geographies in creating DEI impact and sustainability:

- DEI Strategy Development
- DEI Strategic Frameworks for Formal Mentorship and Sponsorship Initiatives
- Strategic Diversity, Equity, and Intentional Inclusion
- Customized Strategic DEI Events and Initiatives
- Launching/Refining Impact of ERGs/BRGs and DEI Councils
- Establishing Diverse Community Impact
- Setting DEI Metrics and Tracking
- Diversity, Equity, and Inclusion Executive Leadership Coaching
- DEI Focused Instructional Design and Facilitation
- And much more...

To find out more about Nika White Consulting services or to access complimentary resources for inclusive leadership, visit:

WWW.NIKAWHITE.COM

To book Dr. Nika White for a speaking opportunity, visit:

WWW.NIKAWHITESPEAKS.COM

NOTES

NOTES

NOTES

Acknowledgments

I'd first like to thank God for sustaining me and giving me such clarity of purpose in this work of DEI.

Thank you to my family and friends, for always extending light, love, and unconditional support, cheering me on when imposter syndrome would start to kick in.

To my client partners, who have trusted me with your most protected assets, your people and your cultures. I'm grateful.

To my NWC teammates and those colleagues who have partnered with me in the business, thank you for believing in and trusting my leadership so that we can collectively achieve impact and not just activity.

To the Forbes Books team for seeing my passion, believing in my voice, and maintaining the integrity of my vision.

To my parents, Jimmy and Sharon Clinkscales, for instilling in me commitment, passion, and hard work.

Finally, I want to acknowledge all the DEI leaders and practitioners that I follow, support, and admire, from both near and far, who commit to this work every day to create more equitable and inclusive societies. Whatever our journey calls us to, it is our collective will, passion, and efforts that move us toward a world where every human can do their best work and live their best lives.

Index

D

I

J

K

Z